I0221654

John M. Buckalew

The Frontier Forts within the north and west Branches of the

Susquehanna River

John M. Buckalew

The Frontier Forts within the north and west Branches of the Susquehanna River

ISBN/EAN: 9783337146399

Printed in Europe, USA, Canada, Australia, Japan

Cover: Foto ©ninafisch / pixelio.de

More available books at **www.hansebooks.com**

THE FRONTIER FORTS

WITHIN THE

North and West Branches of the Susquehanna River,

PENNSYLVANIA.

A REPORT OF THE STATE COMMISSION APPOINTED TO
MARK THE FORTS ERECTED AGAINST THE
INDIANS PRIOR TO 1783,

BY

CAPTAIN JOHN M. BUCKALEW,

A MEMBER OF THE COMMISSION, AND CORRESPONDING MEMBER OF THE
WYOMING HISTORICAL AND GEOLOGICAL SOCIETY.

———————

READ BEFORE THE WYOMING HISTORICAL AND GEOLOGICAL SOCIETY, OCTOBER 4, 1895.
AND REPRINTED FROM THE STATE REPORT, 1896.

WILKES-BARRE, PENN'A
1896.

It was the intention of the Publication Committee of the Wyoming Historical and Geological Society to issue the following valuable paper of Captain J. M. Buckalew, simultaneously with the publication, by the State, of the two volumes entitled "The Frontier Forts," from which they were reprinted. But it was found impossible to procure the plates and maps used in the State Report, and the Committee has been compelled to provide the illustrations from another source. Hence the delay. The illustrations are from plates kindly supplied by Captain Buckalew, and electrotyped by the *Evening Times* of this city.

THE FRONTIER FORTS

WITHIN THE

NORTH AND WEST BRANCHES

OF THE

SUSQUEHANNA RIVER.

BY JOHN M. BUCKALEW

THE FRONTIER FORTS BETWEEN THE NORTH AND WEST BRANCHES.

To the Honorable the Commission appointed by his Excellency, Gov. Robert E. Pattison, under Act of Assembly, approved the 23d day of May, A. D. 1893, to examine and report to the next session of the Legislature upon the advisability of marking by suitable tablets the various forts erected against the Indians by the early settlers of this Commonwealth prior to the year 1783.

This committee, having qualified, met in Harrisburg in November, 1893; after organizing, divided the State into five districts, one to each member to examine and report upon to the body at some time agreed upon. This being the time set, I respectfully submit for your inspection and approval the result of my investigations.

Commencing my labors soon after returning home from Harrisburg, I found my territory, which comprised old Northumberland county, with her ample limits contained fifteen or sixteen of these forts, many of whose sites were unknown to the great mass of our citizens. Three to five generations had passed away since the stirring scenes that made these forts necessary had been enacted; in some cases the descendants of the early settlers had removed or the families died out of the knowledge of the present generation. One would wonder at this was he not acquainted with the settling up of the great West, where, for seventy or more years poured a steady stream of emigrants, who, I am happy to say, have done no discredit to the State rearing them.

Those paying attention to archeology invariably assisted me to the extent of their ability whenever called upon. I am deeply indebted to Col. John G. Freeze, author of History of Columbia County; Hon. John Blair Linn, author of Annals of Buffalo Valley; J. M. M. Gernerd, of Muncy, and publisher-author of Now and Then, for much valuable aid. To that veteran historian, John F. Meginness, of Williamsport, I am deeply indebted for assistance in locating a part of the forts, as well as the information derived from his publications, especially his "Otzinachson," or History of the West Branch Valley; to J. H. MacMinn and Capt. David Bly, of Williamsport, and Capt. R. Stewart Barker, of Lock Haven, for valuable aid; to Wm. Field Shay, Esq., and J. I. Higbee, of Watsontown, for information and aid in locating sites of some of the forts; to David Montgomery, at Fort Rice at Montgomery's for aid; to O B. Melick, Esq., of Bloomsburg, for aid in locating; to M. L. Hendricks, of Sunbury, for gentlemanly aid to the Commission when there; to Dr. R. H. Awl, of the same place, for information to the Commission. We found him a veritable storehouse of knowledge in all pertaining to Fort Augusta, to Sunbury and its surroundings.

I find it impossible to set out the claims of many of these forts to recognition without including the biography in part of some of the most active participants in the stirring events of their date, and consequently, our report will assume greater dimensions than originally expected.

The forts coming within my review according to the decision of the commission, were as follows:

Fort Augusta. At Sunbury, Northumberland county, Pa., on East bank of Main River Susquehanna, and near the junction of its North and West Branches, covering branches and main river.

Fort Jenkins. Located on the north bank of the North Branch of the Susquehanna, in Centre township, Columbia county, about midway between the present towns of Berwick and Bloomsburg.

Fort Wheeler. Located on banks of Fishing Creek, about three miles above present town of Bloomsburg, on B. & S. R. R., in Scott township, Columbia county, at Shew's paper mill.

Fort McClure. Located on bank of river within the present limits of town of Bloomsburg, Columbia county, Penna.

Fort Bosley, or Bosley's Mills. Located at Washingtonville, Derry township, Montour county, in the forks of the Chilisquaqua Creek.

Fort Freeland. Located on the north side of Warrior Run, about four miles east of Watsontown, Northumberland county, and on the line of the W. & W. R. R.

Fort Boone, or Boone's Mills. Located on Muddy Run, near its mouth, between the towns of Milton and Watsontown, and about two miles below the latter, near the West Branch of the Susquehanna, in Northumberland county, Pa.

Fort Swartz. Located on the east bank of the West Branch of the Susquehanna river, in Northumberland county, Pa., about one mile above present town of Milton.

Fort Menninger. Located at White Deer Mills, on the west bank of the West Branch of the Susquehanna and on the north bank of White Deer creek, near the town of White Deer, in Union county.

Fort Brady. Located adjoining the town of Muncy, Lycoming county, south of the built-up portions of the town.

Fort Muncy. Located on railroad about a half mile above Hall's Station, in Lycoming county, and a few hundred yards directly in front of the famous Hall's Stone House of 1769.

Fort Antes. Located on the edge of a plateau overlooking Nippenose Creek, at its mouth and commanding the West Branch of the Susquehanna river, on the south side, opposite the town of Jersey Shore, situated in Lycoming county, near line of P & E. R. R.

Fort Horn. Located on the P. & E. railroad, about midway between Pine and McElhattan Stations, in Clinton county, Pa.

Fort Reid. Located in the town of Lock Haven, Clinton county, Penna., on Water street, in close proximity and east of the Bald Eagle canal. Fortified, spring of 1777.

Fort Rice. At Montgomery's, known in turns by each of these names. Located in Lewis township, Northumberland county, four miles west of Bosley's mills, and two or three miles from site of Fort Freeland.

Respectfully submitted,

JOHN M. BUCKALEW.

THE FORTS.

FORT AUGUSTA—AT SUNBURY.

Was built in 1756, on the east bank of the main river just
below the junction of the North and West branches of the
Susquehanna that here form the main river, the artillery covering the debouchure of the branches, as well as the main
river, at once closing the path by land and movement by water
to the settlements below from an enemy; it stood at the upper
end of the now enterprising town of Sunbury, was a regularly
laid out fort, and when completed, mounted as the returns of
the times show, at least twelve cannon and two swivels; quite
a formidable armament for the time and place; seven blunder-
busses were also included in its armament; it was one of those
military necessities barely acted upon in time.

The causes that led to the building of the fort were: The
French and English were struggling for the supremacy at this
time in America. The English, in our State, had pushed settlements up to the Blue mountains on the north, and were
moving through the passes of the Alleghenies towards Duquesne: the French owned Canada and the Lakes and had an
eye to the ultimate conquest of our State or a part of it. In
pursuance of this object, as they held Duquesne, now Pitts-
burgh, they had fortified Lake Erie at Presqu' Isle, and run
a line of forts by the waters of the Allegheny river, from
Presqu' Isle to Fort Duquesne. The forks of the Susquehanna, after securing their communication with Duquesne attracted their attention; the branches of the Susquehanna, the
one rising in one of the lesser lakes in the State of New York,
the other overlapping some of the branches of the Allegheny,
offered them water communication a part of the distance to
the forks of the Susquehanna. When we take into consideration that Braddock's defeat had occurred but a year before
this and their allies, the Indians, were still elated over this

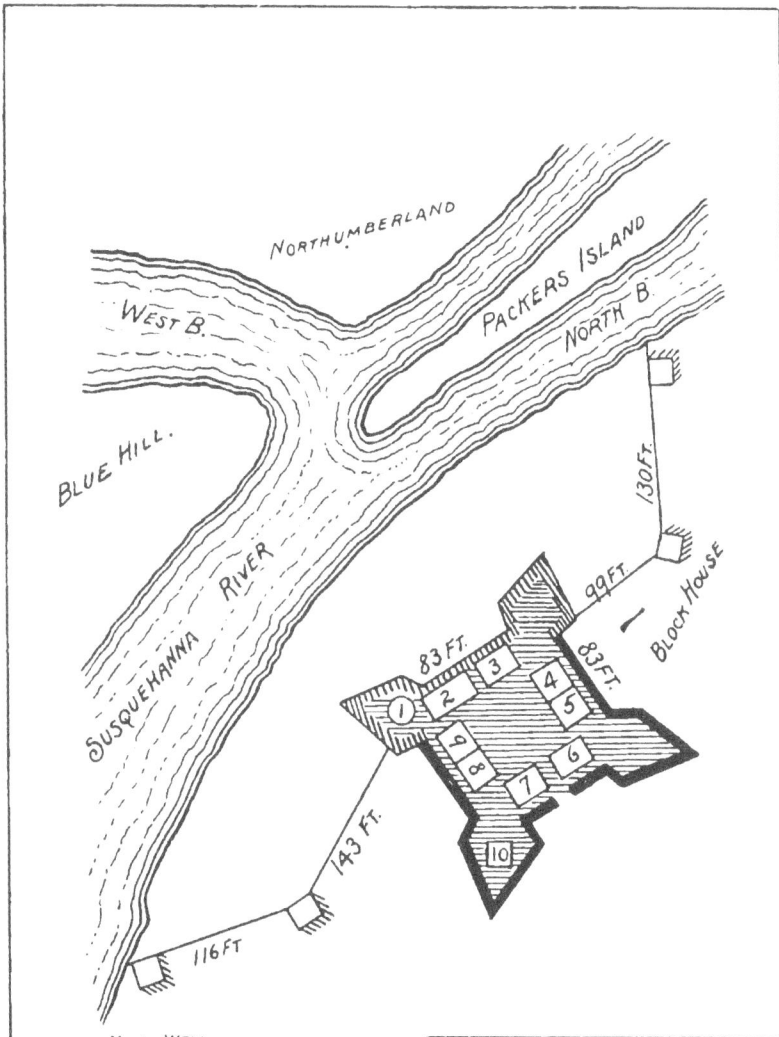

No. 1. WELL
No. 2. OFFICER'S QUARTERS 20×40 FEET.
No. 3. COLONEL'S QUARTERS 18×30 FEET.
No. 4. BARRACKS 25×30 FEET
No. 5. BARRACKS " × " "
No. 6   "   "   " × " "
No. 7   "   "   " × " "
No. 8. SOLDIER'S BARRACKS 25×30 FEET.
No. 9. BARRACKS 25×30 FEET.
No. 10. MAGAZINE.

THE OLD FORT AUGUSTA GUN.

MAP OF FORT AUGUSTA.

great victory and ready for new conquests; the movements of
the French at this time indicate this plainly, as shown by the
Tradition of the Cannon Hole at the Race Ground Island, in
the West Branch, as told the English by the Indians after
peace, was that a party of French and Indians had left the
lake country in the fall of 1756 to make permanent advance to
the forks of the Susquehanna, bringing along three small
brass cannon. Striking the head waters of the Susquehanna
(West Branch), they descended by water to about the mouth
of Loyal Sock creek, where, landing, they sent a reconnoitering
party to the top of the Blue hill overlooking the forks and Fort
Augusta, then partially built. Seeing the advancement of the
fort and the number of men guarding it, considered it impru-
dent to attack and so reported to the main body who, after
consultation, decided to return; as the water was falling, finding themselves encumbered with their cannon, they threw
them in the deep pot hole, or eddy, at the upper end of the old
time race ground island, which has been known as the Cannon
Hole ever since. Fort Augusta continued on the alert for
French aggressions until some time after the capture of Que-
bec by Wolf in 1759, which virtually decided the control of the
Canadas and, of course, of the Indian allies of the French.

The friendly Indians at Shamokin urged Gov. Morris to erect
a strong house at Shamokin for his and their defence, and as a
rallying point for such Indians as were or might become
friendly to the English interests. The Governor was slower to
comprehend the military necessity of the move than the Indians. After considerable delay he finally secured the consent
of the Royal Commissioners and, upon the Assembly voting
£2,000 for the King's use, he directed Colonel William Clapham to recruit a regiment of four hundred men for that purpose; when the regiment was completed he furnished him a
plan of a regular fort to be built on the east bank of the Susquehanna river, at Shamokin. Col. Clapham, after building
Fort Halifax and leaving fifty men to garrison it to keep open
his communications and protect the inhabitants on the upper
part of his route, arrived at Shamokin in July, 1756, after
building a protection for his men and stores, proceeded to exe-
cute the Governor's commands, and before winter, had it quite

secure. Col. Clapham did not remain here a great length of
time after completing the fort, being called away by other duties. He was killed by the Indians in 1763, together with his
family, on Sewickley creek, in Western Pennsylvania. Col.
James Burd, who succeeded him, continued to strengthen the
work, as his interesting journal shows. (See Archives, second
series, Vol. ii, pp. 745-820.) Col. Burd participated in the Bouquet expedition and had command of 582 men. He was in the
battle of Loyal Hanna (Bushy Run) and, after that victory,
accompanied the army to Fort Duquesne.

For the correspondence in the matter, see History of the
Forts, Appendix to Penna. Archives, Vol. xii, first series,
where it is fully collated with references, and shows the mag-
nitude of the undertaking at so great a distance from his base
of supplies, with the difficulties of transportation.

Fort Augusta was at once armed with eight cannon and two
swivels; the number was increased to twelve, or fifteen cannon and two swivels.

Upon the close of the "French and Indian War," notwithstanding the great importance of Fort Augusta as a strategic
point to the Province, a clamor was raised by the "peace at any
price" party of that day, and the fort was partly dismantled.
The condition of affairs in the Province at this time is ably described by Dr. Egle, in his History of Pennsylvania, which
says: "The situation of the frontiers was truly deplorable ow-
ing to the supineness of the Provincial authorities, for the
Quakers who controlled the Government were, to use the lan-
guage of Lazarus Stewart, 'more solicitous for the welfare of
the bloodthirsty Indian than for the lives of the frontiersman.'
In this blind partiality, bigotry and political prejudice they
would not readily accede to the demands of those of a different
religious faith. To them, therefore, was greatly attributable
the reign of horror and devastation in the border counties.
The Government was deaf to all entreaties, and General Am-
herst, commander of the British forces in America, did not hes-
itate to give his feelings an emphatic expression. 'The conduct
of the Pennsylvania Assembly,' he wrote, 'is altogether so in-
fatuated and stupidly obstinate that I want words to express
my indignation thereat.' Nevertheless, the sturdy Scotch-

Irish and Germans of the frontier rallied for their own defence and the entire force of Colonel Bouquet was composed of them."

Fort Augusta, at time of building, held a place of great strategic importance, being far in advance of the English settlements of the Province, holding the only passage by water and blocking the pathway along the river by land, to the pioneer settlements below.

Readily reinforced and provisioned by batteaux from below, the country spreading out fan-like before it, requiring an elaborate system of forts in front of it to restrain it; a safe depot for supplies and the accumulation of a force for aggression, a point where the main Indian paths could be readily reached, and communications kept with them and supply them with the necessary beads and gew-gaws to keep them on friendly terms, or, on the other hand, to restrain them. Here Colonel Hartley drew his supplies in part in his famous march to the destruction of Tioga in 1778, returning by way of the North Branch. Here, Colonel Plunket organized his expedition against Wyoming, ending in the fiasco of Nanticoke and also ending the doughty Colonel's military aspirations.

After the commencement of the Revolution Fort Augusta became the headquarters of this that may be properly termed the military department of the upper Susquehanna. Col. Hunter was appointed county lieutenant and exercised authority here to the close of the war. Col. Hartley, with his regiment was stationed here a part of 1777 and 1778. On the breaking out of the Indians these settlements, which had furnished the main body of their men capable of bearing arms to the Continental army cried loudly for aid. After the battle of Brandywine, Gen. Washington consolidated the 12th Pennsylvania regiment that, by its fierce fighting at Brandywine and other places was almost decimated, with the 3d and 6th Pennsylvania regiments, mustered out the officers and sent them home to help the people organize for defence. Capt. John Brady, Capt. Hawkins Boone and Capt. Samuel Daugherty being among the number. A system of forts were decided upon to cover the settlements as much as they were possibly able to do so, and were designed

1*

to run across the country from near opposite Nescopeck, commencing on the north bank of the North Branch, where was quite a settlement on the river flats; via Meelick's, on Fishing creek, to Bosley's mills, covering most of the settlers on Chillisquaque, to Freeland's mill, on Warrior Run, thence to Widow Smith's mills on west side of West Branch; thence returning to Muncy and thence to Hall's, continuing on up and crossing to Antes Fort; continuing up on the south side of the river to Mr. Reid's, at now Lock Haven. A few of these places were fortified in 1777, but a portion were fortified in the spring of 1778. As the Indians became quite active in the spring of 1778, the military authorities of Fort Augusta were kept very actively engaged. The massacre at Wyoming in that year with the Big Runaway, on the West Branch, deluged Fort Augusta with the destitute and distressed; already overloaded, they were now overwhelmed. The most of these destitute and distressed people soon passing down the river, most of the garrisons were withdrawn. The Indians soon followed and burned everything undefended. At this time the valley of the West Branch presented a pitiable spectacle, which it did not regain to any extent until peace was proclaimed.

It has been claimed by some that at the time of the Big Runaway Col. Hunter lost his head and precipitated matters by withdrawing the garrisons of these forts on the West Branch. To one looking at his exhausted means for defence we cannot see how, as a prudent military man, he could do otherwise. Without means to reinforce the feeble garrisons that were menaced by a foe more powerful than himself, to have left them to their fate would have been improper and likely to have been condemned by those who were so ready to find fault with him for doing the only thing in his power to do as a military head to this department. Colonel Hunter, at this time, had commanded this department fifteen years and knew the country and its people intimately; had become so thoroughly affiliated with their interests as to be one of them; their fears and misfortunes affected him as they did them. What few rays of joy that broke through the black clouds of adversity were as exhilarating to him as to them. He was an openhearted, hospitable, brave, generous man, who eventually spent twenty years of his life in their service and died in 1781, before he saw the full effects of peace, and was buried by the side of the fort he so ably defended, and among the people he worked for and loved so ardently. He was one of the many prominent men who settled in this region.

General Potter, who served in the Continental army and lived in the Buffalo Valley, was a man of great ability, forced by bad health to resign from the Continental army before the close of the Revolution. He was indefatigable in his endeavors to resist the foe and place his people in a safe position of defence. He, too, merits the approbation of the succeeding generations.

Colonel John Kelly and Colonel Hartley are entitled to worthy remembrance for the many acts of military ability shown by them.

Moses Van Campen, whose young manhood developed on the waters of the Fishing creek, detained by the Committee of Safety from the Continental army for the defence of the frontiers, spent the summer of 1777 in Colonel Kelly's regiment in holding Fort Reid and scouting duty, being orderly sergeant of Captain Gaskin's company. In 1778 we find him a lieutenant, and early in the season building Fort Wheeler on the Fishing creek and on scouting duties; in 1779 scouting duties and quartermaster to collect stores for Sullivan's army. Arriving at Tioga he volunteered, with many important scouts intrusted to him, in which he acquitted himself well. In 1780, captured by the Indians, his father, brother and uncle killed, he, Peter Pence and Abram Pike, rising on their captors, killed nine and wounded the only remaining one. This was about fifteen miles below Tioga; 1781 engaged in scouting and looking after tories; winter spent in guarding British prisoners; spring of 1782 marched Robinson's Rangers, of which he was lieutenant, back to Northumberland; after a few day's rest, ordered to rebuild Fort Muncy. Having commenced the work, on arrival of his captain he was sent with a detail of men to the neighborhood of the Big Island, where he was attacked by a large body of Indians led by a white man, when in the fight that ensued, his party were killed or captured, he included among the latter, ran the gauntlet at the Indian towns. Fortune favored him, and he was not recognized as the leader who killed the Indians when a captive until after he was sold to the English. A tedious captivity ensued, enlivened occasionally by practical jokes, etc. He was at last exchanged and returned home, where, after recruiting his health he was sent to assist garrisoning Fort Wilkes-Barre. At this place he remained to the close of the war. Having during his service, built Fort Wheeler and defended it for a time, built Fort McClure and assisted at rebuilding Fort Muncy, besides being actively engaged on frontier duties from the commencement to the close of the war. He removed to the state of New York before 1800 where, after an active life as surveyor and engineer he died, at the advanced age of ninety-two, universally respected.

Visiting with the Forts Commission the ruins of Fort Augusta in the summer of 1894, under the guidance of Mr. M. L. Hendricks, of Sunbury, we found the magazine still there and in good condition. John F. Meginness, in his Otzinachson, or History of the West Branch Valley, page 269, gives a description of it as we saw it: "The magazine was built according to report, on plans of Capt. Gordon, who served as engineer, and to-day is still in a good state of preservation, being the only evidence of the existence of the fort. It is located in a small field about sixty feet south of the brick house known as the 'Hunter Mansion,' and one hundred and sixty-five feet from the river bank. A small mound of earth marks the spot where it may be found, and upon examination an opening in the ground is discovered which is two and a half feet wide. There are twelve four-inch stone steps leading below. On descending these steps the ground space inside the magazine is found to be 10x12 feet, and it is eight feet from the floor to the apex of the arched ceiling. The arch is of brick and commences on an offset purposely made in the wall five feet above the ground floor. The brick are of English manufacture and were transported from Philadelphia to Harris's and then up the river by batteaux. On entering the ancient magazine one is reminded of a huge bake oven; it has been stated that an underground passage led from the magazine to the river, but has been closed up. Although a break or narrow cave-in in the river bank directly opposite the magazine which had existed for years

would indicate that such was the fact, yet there is no evidence
on the inside walls that there ever was such a passage. A recent careful examination failed to show any signs of an opening having existed. The stone basement walls are as solid ap-
parently as when they were first laid. There are no marks or
other evidence whatever that there had been an opening in the
wall or that it had been closed up since the construction of the
magazine." (Query: Would a magazine in a warlike fort have
communication with the outside world.) "There was such a
passage starting from one of the angles of the fort, but it had
no connection with the magazine."

There is but one of the cannon that was formerly mounted
upon the fort known to be in existence. Mr. Hendricks took
the commission to Fire Engine House No. 1 and showed us the
highly prized relic. Dr. R. H. Awl, of Sunbury, furnished J. F.
Meginness its history for his History of the West Branch Valley and a cut of the old cannon. It is securely fastened and
carefully guarded. It is supposed it was thrown in the river
at the time of the great Runaway in 1778, after being spiked.
In 1798 it was reclaimed from the river by George and Jacob
Mantz, Samuel Hahn and George Shoop. After heating, by
burning several cords of hickory wood, they succeeded in drill-
ing out the spiked file. It has had quite a checkered experience, being stolen from one place to another to serve the different political parties, between times hidden in places considered secure until 1834, when Dr. R. H. Awl and ten other
young men of Sunbury made a raid on Selinsgrove at night, secured the much-prized relic and have retained it ever since.
Of the eleven young men engaged in its rescue sixty years ago
the doctor is the only one living to tell the tale of its return.
It is of English make, weighs about one thousand pounds and
has about three and one-half inch bore. A drunken negro
sledged off the ring at the muzzle, out of pure wantonness in
1838.

The Maclay mansion, built by William Maclay, one of the
most prominent citizens of his time, in 1773, is a historic building. The back part of the lot was stockaded during the Revolution. The house is built of limestone and is now owned and
occupied by Hon. S. P. Wolverton, present member of Con-

gress from this district, who prizes it highly for its antiquity and historic reminiscences.

Near here Conrad Weiser built the "Locke house" for Shick-elimy in 1754, the first building in the "Shamokin country," and built for a place to confine refractory Indians. Shick-elimy is said to have at one time exercised almost unlimited control over the Indian tribes, north, west and south. Here the Vice-King died and was buried in 1759. When the grave of Shickelimy was removed some years ago, Mr. M. L. Hendricks, the antiquarian of Sunbury, secured the strings of wampum, the pipe and many other relics that were buried with the Vice-King. He was the father of Logan, the Mingo chief.

The Bloody Spring. The Hon. S. P. Wolverton also owns the land on which this spring is located. Its history, as related by Col. Samuel Miles, is as follows, and shows the constant danger menacing the garrisons of Fort Augusta. In the summer of 1756, I was nearly taken prisoner by the Indians. At about half a mile distant from the fort stood a large tree that bore excellent plums, in an open piece of ground, near what is now called the Bloody Spring. Lieut. S. Atlee and myself one day took a walk to this tree to gather plums. While we were there a party of Indians lay a short distance from us, concealed in the thicket, and had nearly gotten between us and the fort, when a soldier belonging to the Bullock guard not far from us came to the spring to drink. The Indians were thereby in danger of discovery and in consequence thereof fired at and killed the soldier, by which means we got off and returned to the fort in much less time than we were coming out. The rescuing party from the fort found the soldier scalped and his blood trickling into the spring, giving the water a crimson hue, and was ever afterwards called the Bloody Spring. John F. Meginness, who visited this spring a few years ago, says: "This historic spring is located on the hillside. The space occupied by it is about the size of an ordinary town lot, and it looks as if it might have been dug out and the earth taken away with horse and cart. The distance across is about twenty-five feet and has a depth of ten or twelve feet, and then runs out with the declivity. The spring has been gradually filling up and there is no doubt it would flow constantly if it were cleaned out. The spring now only runs over a couple of months in the spring of the year.

The Blue Hill, standing out boldly, opposite Northumberland, is here in bold relief surmounted in our younger days by Mason's observatory overhanging the cliff of some four hundred feet in height; it is now capped by a fine health resort hotel.

The famous thief, Joe Disbury, was tried at Sunbury in 1784 for some of his many misdemeanors, found guilty, sentenced to receive thirty-nine lashes, stand in the pillory one hour, have his ears cut off and nailed to the post, that be imprisoned three months, and pay a fine of £30. The venerable Dr. Awl still shows the place on the old square where punishment was inflicted by the pillory and whipping post. The famous Dr. Plunket, after attaining notoriety as a military leader, took to the bench. As a jurist he dispensed law impartially; as to "rogues," he saw they did not go unwhipped of justice.

FORT JENKINS.

Fort Jenkins was erected in the fall of 1777, or the winter and early spring of 1778. From its size inside the stockades, 60x80 feet, we incline to the former date. Mr. Jenkins, the owner of the house around which the stockade was erected, had been a merchant in Philadelphia, of means, and at this time there was quite a number of settlers within three miles whom he might get to assist at a work of this kind.

If built by Colonel Hartley's men, one would suppose they would have built it larger, to hold Mr. Jenkins' family, the settlers and their families in an emergency, and at least thirty of themselves, and one would also suppose Col. Hartley would have mentioned it or been credited with its building, as he was with Fort Muncy. It was a stockade enclosing the dwelling of Mr. Jenkins, the proprietor of the land, and from present appearances a second building was included, as cellar depression would indicate, it probably dated with the stockading, and had a lookout place on the roof which was a common thing in those perilous times. It is situated on a high bank, or flat, on the North Branch of the Susquehanna and overlooks the river, about twenty rods distant, as well as the country around, about midway between now the thriving towns of Berwick and Bloomsburg, in Columbia county. The first we hear of Fort Jenkins is from Lieut. Moses Van Campen. When building Fort Wheeler he was attacked by Indians, in the month of May, 1778, and running short of ammunition, he sent two men at night across the country about eight miles to Fort Jenkins; they returned next morning before dawn with an ample sup ply. (Life of Moses Van Campen, page 51.)

It was the right flanking defence of the line running from here, on the North Branch to the West Branch, at White Deer and thence to Lock Haven; here it was near the Connecticut settlements in Salem township, now Luzerne county. It covered the river and was a place of importance, and in conjunction with Wheeler, on the Fishing creek, covered the settlers within their line to the river, from ordinary raids.

Mr. Jenkins sold the property to James Wilson, one of the signers of the Declaration of Independence, who, in turn, sold it to Capt. Frederick Hill, who moved upon it and erected a dwelling on the site of Fort Jenkins, where he built and kept a hotel, and in memory of the old fort named it the Fort Jenkins Hotel. In the old days of stage coaches it was a well known hostelry. When he was too old for business his son, Jacob, succeeded him and kept up the reputation of the place, until, by some chance, he became converted among the Methodists, when (having plenty of the sterling material they make good citizens of within him) cut down his sign post, tore out his bar and devoted himself to his farm, which is a fine one, and to the rearing of his family in the paths of rectitude and virtue, in which he was very successful. Here was born his son, Charles F. Hill, now of Hazleton, an archaeologist of considerable note in this region of country, to whom we are indebted for gathering and preserving many of the facts connected with Fort Jenkins. On September 9, 1893, I met Mr. C. F. Hill, at the site of the fort.

He pointed out that the farm house stood upon the site of

the Jenkins house, that the cellar wall was sat on the original
foundation; that the well at the farm house was dug inside the
oaken palisades of the fort during the Revolution, being seventy-five feet deep and down into the limestone rock. Also
where, when a boy, he recollected seeing the remains of the
oak palisades still visible in his time; the place where his
father had shown him the Indians who were killed in the vicinity were buried; the ground where the whites, civilians and
soldiers, who were killed in fights with Indians or died of dis-
ease were buried; some half dozen apple trees yet remaining
of the orchard planted by Mr. Jenkins before the Revolution,
bearing signs of great age, the orchard planted by his grand-
father showing less signs of age. The spot where, in digging
the foundation to the present kitchen attached to the present
farm house he had found the sunken fire place and hearth,
with bricks about six inches square, unlike anything he had
ever seen, supposed they were of English make and had been
brought up the river in boats. He also pointed out where an
island of five acres, as he remembers it, stood in the river so
heavily timbered as to prevent a view from the fort to the
other side, of which not a sign now remains, heavy floods having destroyed it effectually; also, where Nathan Beach's
father's cabin stood, by the North Branch canal, but under the
guns of the fort. The canal passes between the site of the
fort and river at the foot of the plateau on which the
fort stood. Outside the fort stood the cabin of a family whose
name I have dropped; it consisted of at least six persons and is
referred to by Col. Hunter under date of 26 May, 1779, writing
from Fort Augusta, "there has been no mischief done in this
county since the 17th instant; that there was a family of four
persons killed and scalped about twenty-seven miles above
this, on the North Branch opposite to Fort Jenkins. Suppose
there are Indians seen every day one place or another on our
frontiers."

The story of this massacre, as related by Mr. Hill is, the
parents sending two of their children, a boy and girl, to the
neighborhood of Catawissa, for some necessaries, the children
took the path on the hill back of the cabin running parallel
with the river. After proceeding some distance they came to

2

the remains of a recent fire, where mussels from the river had been roasted. Becoming alarmed, they turned back for home, and, on arriving at end of hill overlooking their house, they saw it in flames and Indians disappearing from the clearing into the woods. On descending they found their family they had left in health a short time before, killed and scalped and themselves homeless orphans. This occurred directly opposite the fort and almost within reach of the rifles, but concealed from view of the garrison by the forest of the island and shore. Their first notice came with smoke of the burning cabin, the Indians disappearing as rapidly as they came."

Col. Hunter says, in reference to the removal of Col. Hubley's regiment toward Wyoming: "This leaves Fort Muncy and Fort Jenkins vacant at this critical time, being harvest time. (Vol. xii, Appendix, p. 381.) Col. Hunter, November 27, proposes to send twenty-five men to Fort Jenkins for the support and protection of the distressed inhabitants." (p. 381.) "Col. Ludwig Weltner writes to the Board of War, December 13, 1779, in reference to the posture of several forts, on his taking command. I found Fort Muncy, on the West, and Fort Jenkins, on the East branch, with the magazine at Sunbury, to have been the only standing posts that were occupied. (p. 381.)

"April 2. 1780; the savages, the day before yesterday, took seven or eight prisoners about two miles above Fort Jenkins, and, comparing the condition of things with what it was twelve months before, when the forts were well garrisoned, Col. Hunter says, now we have but about thirty men at Fort Jenkins, which was not able to spare enough men out of the garrison to pursue the enemy that carried off the prisoners." "On the 9th," Col. Weltner writes from Northumberland and says. "I have manned three material outposts, viz: Fort Jenkins, Fort Montgomery (Fort Rice at Montgomery's) and Bosley's Mills. Col. James Potter writes from Sunbury, Sept. 18, 1780, that the enemy burned and destroyed everything in their power and on their going they sent a party and burnt the fort and buildings at Fort Jenkins, which had been evacuated a few days before, on the enemy appearing at Fort Rice."

Nathan Beach, Esq., an old and highly respected as well as widely-known citizen of Luzerne county (in Miner's History of

Wyoming, Appendix, p. 36), says: "In the year 1769 my father removed with his family from the State of New York to the Valley of Wyoming, now Luzerne county, State of Pennsylvania, where he continued to reside within the limits of the said county until the 4th day of July, 1778, the day after the Wyoming Massacre, so-called, when the inhabitants, to wit, all those who had escaped the tomahawk and scalping knife fled in every direction to places of security. About the first of August following, I returned with my father and Thomas Dodson to secure our harvest, which we had left in the fields. While we were engaged in securing our harvest as aforesaid, I was taken prisoner by the Indians and Tories; made my escape the day following. In the fall of the same year, 1778, my father and family went to live at Fort Jenkins (Columbia county, Pa.). I was there employed with others of the citizens and sent out on scouting parties by Capt. Swany (Capt. Isaac Sweeney of Col. Hartley's Eleventh Pennsylvania regiment), "commander of the fort, and belonging to Col. Hartley's regiment of the Pennsylvania line. Continued at said fort until about the first of June, 1779, during which time had a number of skirmishes with the Indians. In May the Indians, thirty-five in number, made an attack on some families that lived one mile from the fort and took three families prisoners, twenty-two in number. Information having been received at the fort, Ensign Thornbury (Ensign Francis Thornbury of the Lieut. Cols. Company afterwards transferred to Third Pennsylvania) was sent out by the captain in pursuit of the Indians with twenty soldiers, myself and three others of the citizens also went, making twenty-four. We came up with them—a sharp engagement ensued, which lasted about thirty minutes, during which time we had four men killed and five wounded out of the twenty-four. As we were compelled to retreat to the fort, leaving our dead on the ground, the Indians took their scalps. During our engagement with the Indians the prisoners before mentioned made their escape and got safe to the fort. The names of the heads of those families taken prisoners as aforesaid were Bartlet Ramey, Christopher Forrow and Joseph Dewey; the first named, Bartley Ramey, was killed by the Indians. Soon after the aforesaid engagement in June, I entered the boat department, boats having been built at Middletown, Dauphin county, called Continental boats made for the purpose of transporting the baggage, provisions, etc., of Genl. Sullivan's army, which was on its march to destroy the Indian towns in the lake country, in the State of New York. I steered one of these boats to Tioga Point, where we discharged our loading and I returned to Fort Jenkins in August, where I found our family. The Indians still continued to be troublesome; my father thought it advisable to leave the country and go to a place of more safety. We left the Susquehanna, crossed the mountains to Northampton county, in the neighborhool of Bethlehem, this being the fall of 1779. Nathan Beach says our family Record says I was born July, 1763, near a place now called Hudson, consequently he was at that time but little past sixteen." Showing the development of the boys of that period into men under the pressure of the circumstances in which they were placed, his case is not an exceptional one.

Fort Jenkins, built in the fall of 1777 or early spring of 1778, was garrisoned by about thirty men under Col. Hartley. Col. Adam Hubley, Jr., who succeeded him, marched the regiment away, when County Lieut. Col. Hunter furnished a few men who, with the citizens of the neighborhood held the fort until the arrival of Col. Ludwig Weltner with the German Battalion about the latter part of 1779, on their return from the Sullivan campaign. After remaining at Wilkes-Barre on guard for some time, Weltner's sturdy Germans held the post until the 5th or 6th of September, 1780, when, on the attack on Fort Rice by 250 or 300 Tories and Indians, the garrison was withdrawn to go to the support of Fort Rice and Fort Augusta.

On failure to capture the fort, the Tories and Indians broke into smaller parties, overrun the country with tomahawk and fire. One large company moved east by end of the Nob Mountain to the river; finding Fort Jenkins abandoned they set fire to it and to the buildings in the neighborhood on the 9th of September; they commenced to cut down the orchard planted by Mr. Jenkins before the Revolution. It is supposed their attention was called from this by news of the approach of Capt. Klader with a company of Northampton county militia, when they suddenly decamped, crossed the river in the neighbor-

MAP OF THE SHARP LOOP MASSACRE

L.V.R.R.

BUCK MOUNTAIN

J.FINK

J.MYERS

CONYNGHAM STATION

NEW TOLL HOUSE

OLD TOLL HOUSE 274

P.WEAVER HOTEL

93

TO HAZLETON

TO MILNESVILLE

A.MCMURTRIE

MRS.SENN 466

CONYNGHAM

J.M.SENN EST

T.CAWLEY

CEM CHRIST.CH ODD FELLOWS HALL 337

J.ENGLE

J.CRABLEY

106

N.E.BIRD

A.ROTE

J.HOUSTKNECHT

SEYBERTSVILLE P.O.

258

N.KEMBLE

J.S.BALLIETT

C.TRESHOLD

N.S

SCHOOL

P.SHAFER

N.SNYDER

MRS.OWENS

PREARICK

J.CAUGHMAN

W.SHERRY

S.BENNER

W.HABE

W.DISTELHURST PAINT SHOP

J.HOUSEKNECHT

J.GULP

P.O.

247

234

731 KLADER'S GRAVEX 225

J.HINES

MRS.TROY

E.ROTE

S.HOUSEKNECHT

J.J.SHAFER

296

J.KNEELEY

S.WAGNER

J.WAGNER

J.KAMELY

240

D.SANTEE

D.REARICK

J.GETTING

TIMES ENG.DEPT.

hood of now Berwick, went on to Sugarloaf, in Luzerne
county, where they ambuscaded the militia, killed or captured
the greater portion of them, broke up the expedition, relieved
their Tory friends of fear of capture and expulsion of their
families. The Indians are said to have passed up east of Wyoming to their homes in the lake country. Fort Jenkins, from
the many raids in its neighborhood, shows to have been much
in the way of the Indians.

FORT WHEELER.

Lieut. Moses Van Campen says, " Early in the month
of April, 1778, he was ordered to go with his men up the
North Branch of the Susquehanna river to the mouth of Fishing creek and follow up this three miles to a compact settlement, located in that region, and build a fort for the reception
of the inhabitants in case of an attack from the Indians.
News had come thus early of their having visited the outer
line of settlements and of their committing depredations, so
that terrified messengers were arriving almost daily, bringing
the sad news of houses burned, victims scalped and of families
carried into captivity.

"It was no time to be idle; a few days, it might be a few hours,
and the savage might be amongst those whom he was appointed
to guard and repeat these scenes of cruelty and blood. He and
his men, his command of twenty men, who, as well as himself,
were familiar with the country, expert in the use of the rifle
and acquainted with the Indian modes of warfare, without delay they entered vigorously upon the work, selecting a site for
the fort on the farm of Mr. Wheeler (hence, when completed, it
was called Fort Wheeler). It was built of stockades and sufficiently large to accommodate all the families of the neighborhood. Anticipating an early approach of the foe, they worked
with a will to bring the fort to completion or at least into a
condition that would afford some protection in case of an attack. The Indians, in approaching the border settlements,

usually struck upon the head waters of some of the streams upon which settlers were located and followed them down through valley or mountain defile until they came near a white man's house, when they would divide so as to fall in small companies upon different habitations at the same time. "Before the fort was completed a runner came flying with the speed of the wind to announce the approach of a large party of savages. The inhabitants gathered into the fort with quick and hasty rush, taking with them what valuables they could, and leaving their cheerful homes to the undisputed sway of the enemy. Very soon the Indians came prowling around under cover of the woods and all at once, with wild yells, burst forth upon the peaceful farmhouses of the settlement. Fortunately, the inmates were not there to become victims of the tomahawk and scalping knife. From the elevated position of the fort the inhabitants could see their dwellings entered, their feather beds and blankets carried out and scattered around with frantic cries and very soon after the flame and smoke leap to the tops of their houses and, finally, the whole settle down into a quiet heap of ashes. The Indians spent most of the day in pillaging and burning houses, some of them made an attack on the fort but to little purpose. Van Campen and his men were actively engaged in preparing for a vigorous defence in case of an attack to storm their unfinished works. They were successful in surrounding the fort at a distance of four rods with a barricade "made with brush and stakes, the ends sharpened and locked into each other so that it was difficult to remove them and almost impossible for one to get through. The Indians, seeing this obstruction, were disposed to fire at them from a distance, and keep concealed behind the bushes. Their shots were promptly returned and a brisk firing was kept up all the time till evening. It was expected that the Indians would renew the attack the next morning and, as the ammunition of the fort was nearly expended, Van Campen sent two of his men to Fort Jenkins, about eight miles distant, on the Susquehanna, who returned next morning before dawn of day with a plentiful supply of powder and lead. The remaining hours of darkness were spent in running bullets and in making needed preparation for the encounter they were looking for on the approaching day. They judged from what they knew of the superior force of the enemy and from the activity already displayed that the struggle would be severe." In the morning they found the enemy had disappeared. "The Indians, not liking the preparations made to receive them, retired, leaving blood on the ground, but nothing else that would indicate their loss. But the Indians, not satisfied with this visit made another attempt to surprise this fort in the month of June. On one evening in the month of June," says Lieut. Van Campen, "just at the time when the women and girls were milking their cows, a sentinel called my attention to a movement in the bushes not far off, which I soon discovered to be a party of Indians making their way to the cattle yard. There was no time to be lost. I immediately selected ten of my sharpshooters and, under cover of a rise of ground, crept between them and the milkers. On ascending the ridge we found ourselves within pistol shot of our lurking foes. I fired first and killed the leader; this produced an instant panic among the party, and they all flew away like a flock of birds. A volley from my men did no further execution; it only made the woods echo with the tremendous roar of their rifles; it sounded such an unexpected alarm in the ears of the honest dairy women that they were still more terribly frightened than the Indians. They started upon their feet, screamed aloud and ran with all their might, fearful lest the enemy should be upon them. In the mean time the milk pails flew in every direction and the milk was scattered to the winds. The best runner got in first." Lieut. Van Campen appears to have made Fort Wheeler his headquarters this season when not engaged in scouting. After the Sullivan campaign, in the fall of 1779. when Van Campen returned to Fort Wheeler, his father living there—leaving there late in March, 1780.

Fort Wheeler, the traditions of the many descendants of the men who occupied the fort say, was not abandoned but held by hardy settlers, when not garrisoned by troops and that it is the only one of its date of the line in front of Fort Augusta that was not destroyed. Of couse, I do not include McClure, Rice or Swartz, as they were built later. Near here lived Peter Meelick, who served as one of the committee of safety

for this Wyoming township from its institution until super-
ceded by another system.

There is nothing to-day to indicate where the fort stood
except the spring is there. Mr. William Creveling, who owns
the property, says many years ago he ploughed up the fire
place.

O. B. Melick, Esq., of Bloomsburg, says the place his grand-
father, the Peter Meelick above named, and his father fixed
upon as the site of Fort Wheeler is the same as that shown by
Mr. Creveling. Mr. Theodore McDowell, since dead, showed
the same site as the one he and his comrades when boys used
to visit as the remains of Fort Wheeler. The grave yard,
where the soldiers and others were buried, about thirty rods
from the site, I regret to say, is not cared for. There is not a
dissenting voice as to the site, but a unanimity rarely found.

Mr. Isaiah Wheeler, on whose land the fort was built, and
whose dwelling the stockades enclosed, was a settler who came
here from the State of New Jersey, and some accounts say he
died and was buried here. Col. Joseph Salmon, a man of
prominence as a scout and of extraordinary courage in these
times, when examples of courage were not rare, married one
of his daughters. It is said an open manly rivalry existed between Van Campen and Salmon for her hand, when Salmon
distanced the lieutenant and won the damsel.

Mr. Joseph Crawford, an old and respected citizen of Orangeville, says his father, John Crawford, was born in Fort
Wheeler soon after its completion in 1778, being the second
white child born in this vicinity.

McCLURE'S FORT

Col. Freeze says, the year 1777 and the next four or five following, were years of great activity and danger in the Indian
fighting in and about what was originally Columbia county.
The regular military authorities had done their best to protect
the frontiers of the Pennsylvania settlements, but they had

few officers and fewer men to spare from the Federal army, and therefore, the defense of the settlements fell upon the local heroes and heroines of the Forts of the Susquehanna.

A chain of forts, more or less protective had been constructed, reaching from the West Branch to the North Branch of the Susquehanna, comprising Fort Muncy, Fort Freeland, Fort Montgomery, Bosley's Mills, Fort Wheeler and Fort Jenkins. The great war path through the valley, known as the "The Fishing Creek Path," started on the flats, near Bloomsburg, on the North Branch, up Fishing creek to Orangeville, on to near Long Pond, now called Ganoga Lake, thence across to Tunkhannock creek.* It was on this very path that Van Campen, the most prominent Indian fighter on the North Branch was captured, in 1780, and no man better than he knew the great necessities of the section.

The destruction of Fort Jenkins in 1780 had exposed the right flank of the protecting forts and the Indian marauders made wild work among our defenseless frontiers. On his (Van Campen's) return from captivity he assisted in organizing a new force, repairing the forts dismantled or abandoned, and also stockaded the residence of Mrs. James McClure, and the place was thereafter known as McClure's Fort. It is on the north bank of the North Branch of the river Susquehanna, and is reported to have occupied the exact site of the present dwelling house of the late Douglas Hughes, below Bloomsburg, about one mile above the mouth of Fishing creek. It was an accessible point and gave the command of the military line across the river valley. It became the headquarters for stores and expeditions, and was an important point so long as it was necessary to maintain fortifications on the river.

It does not seem to have ever been formally attacked, but there are traditions of lurking savages and hurried embarkings upon boats and canoes and the protection of the wide Susquehanna.

How thrilling soever these adventures may have been they are now forgotten.

NOTE.—Col. Freeze is mistaken ; the Indians with Van Campen and Pence, followed the path up the east branch of Fishing Creek, known as Huntington Creek, and in Huntington township, fired on Col. John Franklin's men, slightly wounding Capt. Ransom, as related by Moses Van Campen. J. M. B.

"Time rolls his ceaseless course; the race of yore,
Who danced our infancy upon their knee,
And told our marvelling boyhood legends store
Of their strange ventures happ'd by land or sea,
How are they blotted from the things that be!

FORT BOSLEY, OR BOSLEY'S MILLS.

Fort Bosley was situated in the forks of the Chillis-
quaqua, at Washingtonville, Derry township, Montour
county, and was the grist mill of a Mr. Bosley, who moved
here from Maryland a few years before the Revolution, bringing his slaves with him. He built the mill, it is said, in 1773;
it is supposed he fortified (stockaded) the mill in 1777; upon
the Indians becoming troublesome it was garrisoned by troops
and recognized by the military authorities as of importance.
After the fall of Fort Freeland it became more so, holding the
forks of the Chillisquaque and defending the stream below it.

The Chillisquaque Valley and its surroundings are among
the most beautiful in the State. At Washingtonville, the main
stream is formed by one considerable branch coming from the
Muncy Hills, following through the rich lime stone lands to
the south. The east branch here joins it, making a fine stream
that then flows southwesterly to the river. This great scope
of fine arable lands attracted settlers early, Bosley's Mills became a necessity, and, situated as it was, within the forks
about sixty to eighty rods above the junction of the branches,
on the east bank of the North Branch of these streams. It
soon became widely known; roads and paths led to it as a central point, and on the Indians becoming troublesome and the
mill fortified, it became a haven of refuge at which the wives
and families could be placed in safety at alarms, while the
husband and father scouted for intelligence of the foe or defended the fort. As Bosley's Mills do not appear to have had
a heavy garrison of troops (twenty men at most) at any time,
the garrison was most probably augmented by the near settlers, of which there was quite a number. It must have been

strong, as we have no account of any attack on the place, lying as it does below the great war path through or over the Muncy Hills, it must have been looked upon by the foe as strong.

Col. Hunter to Prest. Reed, dated Fort Augusta, June 26, 1779, says: "Your favor of ye 2d Inst. I received by Mr. Martin and I am sorry to acquaint you it was not in my power to send any of the Ranging Company to assist at Guarding the stores up here from Estherton, as what few men Capt. Kemplon had under his command was stationed at Bosley's Mills on Chilisquaqua." (See Penna. Archives, vol. vii, p. 510.)

Lieut. Col. Weltner to Board of War, dated Northumberland, April 9, 1780, says: "I have this moment received an express from the West branch, about 12 miles from this Town that the Indians have killed and scalped one man and two children, took one woman prisoner, but she happily made her escape from them in the night. The country is very much alarmed, and likely to go to the flight as they cannot be supplied with provisions, ammunition or flints, as these commodities being so very scarce. I have manned three material outposts, viz: Fort Jenkins, Fort Montgomery and Bosley's Mills. It is out of my power to scatter my men any more, as I have scarcely as many in Town as will man 2 pieces of artillery."

The site of the old mill is recognized readily by the race and mill site and is on the land of Jesse Umstead, Jr., at the lower end of the built up town of to-day. The head race has been continued on across the road and utilizes the old dam site and head race for a modern mill.

FORT RICE.

Fort Rice, at Montgomery's, sometimes written of by one name by the military and other authorities and at another by the other until it was supposed to indicate two separate forts. It is located in Lewis township, Northumberland county, Pa.

In 1769 William Patterson patented seven hundred acres of land on which Fort Rice was situated. On account of its handsome appearance and the fertility of its soil he named it

Paradise. Meginness is correct in saying "For rural beauty, fertility of soil and charming surroundings, with healthfulness, it is not excelled by any district in the United States, and the name Paradise was worthily bestowed." The country is gently rolling and under a high state of cultivation. Neat farm mansions with capacious barns are seen in all directions, and what adds to the beauty of the scene are the open groves of oak and other hard wood, free from underbrush, and a regularity almost equal to being planted by the hand of man, among which scores of gray squirrels may be seen sporting in the woods without fear of the pot hunters or poachers. Mr. Patterson exchanged this Paradise farm with John Montgomery, of Paxtang, in 1771, for his farm in that settlement. The descendants of John Montgomery still reside on these lands. The Montgomery family became widely known for their ability and integrity. At the time of the capture of Fort Freeland, July 28, 1779, John Montgomery living here, heard the firing; mounting two of his young sons on horses he sent them to the top of a hill to "learn the cause of the firing. On arriving at the brow of the hill overlooking the creek they discovered the fort on fire and a fight raging in the timber some distance below. They returned and reported what they had seen; he loaded up his family in a wagon, with what provision and clothing they could carry and hurriedly drove across the country to the cabin of William Davis. After informing him what was going on he gathered up his family and proceeded to Fort Augusta."—(Meginness.)

The Indians burned Mr. Montgomery's house; he took his family to Paxtang, where they remained to the close of the war. The Indians burned the house and everything; in consequence of the fall of Fort Freeland it became necessary to fill its place by another. McClung's place, which, I understand, was between Freeland and the Montgomery farm, was first selected, but it was decided to be impracticable, when, finally the Montgomery farm was selected, and here Captain Rice, of Col. Weltner's German Regiment, erected it in the fall and winter of 1779 and 80. It was built around and enclosed the fine spring at the burned residence of John Montgomery, and remains to-day a lasting tribute to the excellency of the

FORT RICE, AT MONTGOMERY'S,
NORTHUMBERLAND COUNTY

work of Capt. Rice's Pennsylvania Germans. First, building a
stockade for security they completed it, building it out of sur-
face limestone. They occupied and defended it ably. The
only attack made on the fort itself we have any record of occurred in the beginning of September, 1780.   A letter from Col.
Samuel Hunter, at Sunbury, Sept. 21, 1780, found in Vol. viii,
p. 567, Penna. Archives, saying: "We were alarmed by a large
party of the enemy making their appearance in our county on
the 6th inst. They came first to a small fort that Col. Weltner's troops had erected on the headwaters of the Chilisquake,
called Fort Rice, about thirteen miles from Sunbury (17), when
the German Regiment marched off the enemy attacked the
fort about sundown and fired very smartly. The garrison returned the fire with spirit, which made them withdraw a little
off, and in the night they began to set fire to a number of
houses and stacks of grain which they consumed. In the
meantime our militia had collected to the number of one hundred men under the command of Col. John Kelly, who marched to the relief of the Garrison, and arrived there next day.
The people in the Garrison acquainted Col. Kelly that there
must be two hundred and fifty or three Hundred of the Enimy,
which he did not think prudent to engage without being
Reinforced. The confusion this put the inhabitants in, it was
not easy to collect a party equal to fight the savages. I immediately sent off an express to Col. Purdy on Juneate whom
I heard was marching to the Frontiers of Cumberland County
with the militia, he came as quick as possible to our assistance
with one Hundred and ten of the militia and about Eighty
Volunteers, which was no small Reinforcement to us. Genl.
Potter Just coming home from camp at this critical time came
up to Sunbury and took command of the party that went in
Quest of the Enimy. But previous to his marching, dis-
charge the Volunteers as he concluded by the information he
had received from spyes we had out that the enemy did not
exceed one Hundred and fifty and that they had withdrawn
from the inhabitants to some Remote place. General Potter,
However, marched on to Muncy Hills, but was a little Baffled
by the information of their route and did not come on their
track till the 13th and followed on about 50 miles up fishing

creek, the road the enemy took, but finding they had got too far ahead returned here the 17th inst. The enemy got but one scalp and one prisoner (The Colonel did not know of their having committed the Sugarloaf Massacre when he wrote). We all concluded the enimy had gone off, but on the 18th there was a small party made their appearance on the West Branch about fourteen miles above this place, they killed one man and wounded another, and killed their horses they had in the plow, which plainly shows they have scattered into small parties to Harras the inhabitants, which I am afraid will prevent the people from getting crops put in the ground this fall. When the German Regiment marched off from here I give orders for the Frontiers Companys to embody and keep one-fourth of the men Constantly Reconnoitering. After garrisoning Fort Jenkins, Fort Rice, and Fort Schwartz with twenty men in each of them, this was the only method I could think of encouraging the people as we were left to our own exertions. Only about thirty of Capt. McCoys company of Volunteers from Cumberland County, until the 10th Inst., that two companies of militia came here from the same county in the whole about eighty men. When I received the intelligence of a large party of savages and tories coming against Fort Rice, I give orders to evacuate Fort Jenkins as I did not look upon it to be tenable, which is since burned by the Enimy, and would have shared the same had the men staid there on act. of the Buildings that were adjoining it, &c."

As to the numbers attacking Fort Rice, Genl. Potter (Vol. viii, p. 563), says: "Since I wrote the above I am informed by Capt. Robeson that a large body of the enemy crossed the Moncey Hills near one Evses and went up the Moncey Creek so that it is leekly (likely) that the number that was down amounted to 300 men—they carried off a large number of Cattle and Horses."

John Montgomery returned with his family on the return of peace. Finding the buildings of his farm destroyed and a good strong stone house supplying its place; he at once occupied the fort, which, with additions, made him a comfortable home for years. Capt. Rice leaving the country, Montgomery remained and it soon became known as Montgomery's fort. The

old actors in the bloody drama enacted in this region having
passed away, Fort Rice was forgotten except as found in the
old records, which placed it thirteen miles from Sunbury and
on the head waters of the Chillisquaque—both erroneous. Fort
Rice was lost as to site to the present generation. After considerable research I became satisfied Fort Rice and Montgomery must mean the same place.

Hon. John Blair Linn, of Bellefonte, at this time sent me a
newspaper cutting, recording an examination of the subject
by J. F. Wolfinger, of Milton, in about 1885 (since dead). I
have found his statement correct in the main and here present
it: "Our ancestors and first settlers on the West and North
branches of the Susquehanna River had two great runaway
times from the Indians. The first took place in 1778 and the
second one in 1779.   *   *   *   *   John F. Montgomery must certainly have known how and why this stone
building was built over his spring, but as he died in November, 1792, and left no writings with any person to show that
the German Battalion had built it and had a fort and barracks
standing close by his spring (falling into the error that there
was a Fort Rice and a Fort Montgomery close together, he
mistook the defences erected to protect the soldiers and their
arms and commissary while building Fort Rice for the Fort
Montgomery which Rice is). The knowledge of these facts
was entirely unknown to the coming generations of people in
this beautiful region of country called Paradise, and, hence,
a great many different stories very naturally arose as to when
the old stone building in question was built and by whom it
was built and why it had small port holes in its walls and the
like. July 13, 1885. On this day I visited this old Fort Montgomery or Rice ground, accompanied by my old friend, the
Hon. David B. Montgomery, a grandson of the above John F.
Montgomery, and who, I mean David B. M. has for many years
resided about a hundred and fifty yards south of the spot.
Spring House Buildings—A Grand relic. This building is 26x
23 feet outside measurement and is two stories (and an Attic
of 4 feet) high, being 22 feet high from the ground up to its
square on the west side and on a part of its northern end, it is
now used as, and forms in its lower story a splendid spring

house for keeping milk, cream, butter, meats and the like in a very nice and cool condition and it afforded me a good deal of pleasure to have a drink from its clear, cool and refreshing waters.

"The walls of the fort are two feet thick and are composed of rather small dull colored limestone, as no quarries were open at that early day to get stones of a large size and of a clear strong blue color. But its walls are still solid and in a very good condition, considering their age and the hasty manner in which Capt. Rice's German soldiers made them. The door to the spring was and still is in the south end of the building and it had when built in 1779 a wooden stairway that extended from the ground on its eastern side up to the second story, where there was another door for the purpose of storing away there for safe keeping such things as Capt. Rice and his men needed for their use and comfort. But this stairway is gone long ago and the doorway on the second story was also changed long ago into a window, but on the east side it had and still has two windows with twelve panes of glass in each window and all the windows were of the old-fashioned sort, $7\frac{1}{2}$x$8\frac{1}{2}$ inches in size, but one or two of these smaller sized windows have been walled shut with bricks. The northern end of the second story (third story or attic) still has two small port holes made there, no doubt, to enable soldiers standing there to stick their guns through the holes and fire at any Indians that might come there with an evil design, but it is probable that every other side of the building had smaller port holes for this same purpose, but they are all gone now excepting the two just noticed. Mr. Henry Raup, who lives in a fine two-story brick house on the east side of the spring house, called my attention to the fact that a smooth-faced stone in the central part of the southern end wall and about eighty feet above the ground, contained on its face the letters W. R. that were so thinly cut into the stone as to make them after so long a time now have but a faint appearance. As W. and R. are the initials of Capt. William Rice, I now found the evidence strong enough to satisfy me that Fort Rice, Montgomery, you can call it now by either of those names just as you please, actually stood here and nowhere else, on the west side of the road

that runs in front of Raup's house up north to and beyond Tur-
botville. Some time after John F. Montgomery had returned
from his runaway from the Indians, he built a stone addition
to the northern end of the above described spring house (fort)
building, an addition large enough to make a fine eating
room for his family and work hands, and then to make things
handy for the women he cut a hole through the wall of the fort
and put a door there to go into the spring house for milk,
butter, &c. This additional room was torn away long ago and
the above doorway was walled up again but a portion of the
plastering of this room still sticks to the northern wall of the
old fort. Capt. Rice's old building aforesaid thus forms a
grand and very interesting relic of our olden time building
that every man in the county should be proud of and feel a
great pleasure in visiting." I visited the place in 1894 with
James I. Higbee, of Watsontown, and Mr. Yarrington, of the
same place and secured a picture of probably the best preserved fort of its date in the State. I found it two stories and
an attic of four feet or more at the square of the building,
could recognize the old port holes in the walls of the second
story. The old-fashioned chimney was in the northern end,
the spring covered about half the space inside the walls of the
lower story. We hung "Old Glory" out of one of the old port
holes, I suppose the first time since the close of the Revolution.
Capt. Rice's name was Frederick William Rice.

FORT FREELAND.

The sad history of this death trap is well and widely
known, on Warrior run, about four miles east of Watsontown and one mile east of well-known Warrior Run church;
it was stockaded in the fall of 1778 by Jacob Freeland and
his neighbors, enclosing a large two-story log house of
Jacob Freeland, as many of the descendants of the early settlers still live in this region and the bloody ending of the place
has kept it well in remembrance. Jacob Freeland here built a
mill in 1773 and 1774, having brought the iron from New Jer-

3

sey. Mr. Enoch Everitt, of Watsontown, now owns the fine
farms on which it was located. A depression on the yard to
the large brick farm house marks the cellar to the site of the
old Freeland house. A fine spring of water near the house is
still used by the farm house of to-day. In Vol. xii, Penna. Archives, p. 364, is found the recollections of Mary V. Derickson,
born in the Fort Freeland, written in 1855, seventy-five years
after the occurrence, but is remarkably clear. John Blair
Linn, in his Annals of Buffalo Valley, and John F. Meginness,
in his "Otzinachson," give us full particulars, drawn largely
from the Archives.

Mary V. Derickson writes: "Sir: In compliance with your
request, I will give (so far as my memory will serve) all the account of the early settlers and occupants of Fort Freeland.
The fort was situated on the Warrior run creek, about $4\frac{1}{2}$
miles above where it empties into the Susquehanna river. In
the year 1772, Jacob Freeland, Samuel Gould, Peter Vincent,
John Vincent and his son, Cornelius Vincent, and Timothy
Williams, with their respective families cut their way through
and settled within some two miles of where the fort was afterwards built. They were from Essex county, New Jersey.
Jacob Freeland brought the irons for a grist mill, and in the
years 1773 and 1774 built one on Warrior Run. There were
several more families moved up from the same place, and they
lived on friendly terms with the Indians until '77, when they
began to be troublesome and to remove their own families, in
the summer of '78, they had to leave the country, and when
they returned in the fall they picketed (stockaded) around a
large two-story log house (which had been built by Jacob
Freeland for his family), enclosing half an acre of ground; the
timbers were set close and were about twelve feet high;
the gate was fastened by bars inside. Into this fort, or
house, the families of Jacob Freeland, Sen., and Jacob Freeland, Jr., John Little, Michael Freeland, John Vincent, Peter
Vincent, George Pack, Cornelius Vincent, Moses Kirk, James
Durham, Samuel Gould, Isaac Vincent and David Vincent, all
gathered and lived there that winter. In November George
Pack, son of George Pack, was born, and on the 20th May,
George, son of Isaac Vincent, was born, on the 10th of Febru-

ary, 1779, I was born. My father was Cornelius Vincent. In the spring of '79, the men planted corn but were occasionally surprised with the Indians, but nothing serious occurred until the 21st day of July, as some of them were at work in the corn field back of the fort, they were attacked by a party of Indians, about nine o'clock, A. M. and Isaac Vincent, Elias Freeland and Jacob Freeland, Jr., were killed and Benjamin Vincent and Michael Freeland were taken prisoners. Daniel Vincent was chased by them but he outran them and escaped by leaping a high log fence. When the Indians surprised them, Ben. Vincent (then ten years of age) hid in a furrow, but he thought he would be more secure by climbing a tree, as there was a woods near, but they saw him and took him a prisoner. He was ignorant of the fate of the others until about two o'clock P. M., when an Indian thrust a bloody scalp in his face and he knew it was his (and my) brother's Isaac's scalp. Nothing again occurred until the morning of the 29th about daybreak, as Jacob Freeland, Sen., was agoing out the gate he was shot and fell inside of the gate. The fort was surrounded by about three hundred British and Indians, commanded by Capt. McDonald. There were but 21 men in the fort and but little ammunition. Mary Kirk and Phoebe Vincent, commenced immediately and run all their spoons and plates into bullets; about nine o'clock there was a flag of truce raised, and John Little and John Vincent went out to capitulate, but could not agree. They had half an hour given to consult with those inside; at length they agreed that all who were able to bear arms should go as prisoners, and the old men and women and children set free, and the fort given up to plunder. They all left the fort by 12 o'clock P. M. Not one of them having eaten a bite that day and not a child was heard cry or ask for bread that day. They reached Northumberland, eighteen miles distant, that night and there drew their rations, the first they had that day. When Mrs. Kirk heard the terms on which they were set free she put female clothes on her son William, a lad of 16, and he escaped with the women. Mrs. Elizabeth Vincent was a cripple; she could not walk. Her husband John Vincent, went to Capt. McDonald and told him of her situation, and said if he had a horse that the Indians had taken from his son Peter the week before that she could ride about daylight next morning. The horse came to them; he had carried his wife to the lower end of the meadow, where they lay and saw the fort burned, and it rained so hard that night that she laid mid side in the water; when the horse came he stripped the bark off a hickory tree and plaited a halter, set his wife on and led it to Northumberland, where there were wagons pressed to take them on down country.

After the surrender of the fort Capts. Boone and Daugherty arrived with thirty men; supposing the fort still holding out they made a dash across Warrior run, when they were surrounded. Capt. Hawkins Boone and Capt. Samuel Daugherty, with nearly half the force were killed; the remainder broke through their enemies and escaped. Thirteen scalps of this party were brought into the fort in a handkerchief. Soon after this the fort was set fire to and burned down. The killed of the garrison and Boone's party, from best information, to be arrived at amounted to about twenty men, but two such men as Boone and Daugherty in such times were of more value to such a community than many common men.

Thus ended Fort Freeland. Robert Covenhoven, the famous scout and Indian killer of the West Branch, had passed down ahead of this party of Tories and savages, giving notice of their approach, but it is said Fort Freeland did not get notice. Ammunition was hard to get, almost impossible sometimes to procure, which may account for Fort Freeland being so short that the women had to run up their spoon and "pewter" plates, but one would suppose, if there was any head to the garrison after the attack of a few days before, when their loss was three killed and two captured, he would have caused them to be better prepared for another attack.

Each succeeding generation on the Warrior run since the fall of Fort Freeland has pursued up the site of the place that no doubts exist in regard to it.

The effect of the fall of Fort Freeland was disastrous to this region, accompanied as it was with the death of Boone, Daugherty and their brave comrades, and the desertion of Boone's Mills as a post of defence. It entirely uncovered Fort Augusta to the inroads of the enemy. Bosley's Mills alone, with

its small garrison standing on the defensive on one flank liable
to be overthrown when any considerable force of the enemy
appeared before it. Colonel Hunter, holding his base with a
force so feeble as to warrant a less courageous commander in
calling in every man and gun for the protection of Augusta, as comparatively few persons remained to protect
in his front, but holding what he had left. In
November the German Battalion was sent him, count-
ing about one hundred and twenty men, with which he
secured his base, built Fort Rice and garrisoned it, and
built Fort Swartz and also garrisoned it, as well as Fort
Jenkins with thirty men,—with ten to fifteen militia at Bosley's Mills, and a few of the inhabitants to hold Wheeler,
eighty to ninety men in all, besides his garrison of Augusta.
At this date his left flank had been contracted from now Lock
Haven to Milton, with his right weak but intact. Affairs did not
improve much in this department to the close of the war in
1780. The right flanking fort was destroyed by the troops
being withdrawn in an emergency, and some time elapsed before the flank was again protected by Fort McClure, at now
Bloomsburg.

BOONE'S MILLS.

Boone's Fort was erected on Muddy run, a short distance
from the West Branch of the Susquehanna, on the east
bank. It was a grist mill stockaded and owned by Capt.
Hawkins Boone (a cousin to the famous Daniel Boone),
and, according to Linn's Annals of Buffalo Valley, came originally from Exeter, Berks county. Soon after the consolida-
tion of the 12th regiment, Pennsylvania Line, into the 3d and
6th, Capt. Boone, Capt. Brady and Capt. Daugherty were mustered out of service and sent, at the urgent request of the
people of the West Branch to lead their defence. Boone stockaded his mill and was assisted by his neighbors and troops in
defending it. A large, hardy, brave, generous man, he appears to have been highly respected by those knowing him

His fall at Fort Freeland, in 1779, was a serious loss to the community, who looked to good results from his ability and experience; a confidence that was abruptly terminated by his bloody, but soldierly death, attempting to rescue his fellow man.

Probably his loss was more of a public calamity than any man in the valley except his comrade in arms, Capt. John Brady.

In rebuilding the Kemmerer (Boone) mill, the men employed dug down to the old foundations of the Boone mills, showing the present mills occupying the same site. It is about midway between Milton and Watsontown. The Pennsylvania Archives, Linn's Annals and Meginness' Otzinachson all show his ability and courage and the loss to the community by his death, as well as his assistant, Capt. Daugherty. After Boone's death his fortifications are not heard of.

FORT SWARTZ.

Fort Swartz was built on the east bank of the West Branch, at the old Ferry, about a mile above Milton, a log structure, named in honor of Lieut. Christian Godfried Swartz, of Col. Weltner's German Battalion, who stockaded and defended it. It was built after the destruction of the forts above it on the river. It covered the river and its small garrison did some scouting duty. It was one of the three forts left standing from the North Branch to the West in the spring of 1780, viz: Wheeler, Rice and Swartz. It does not appear to have ever been attacked but was a sturdy little sentinel to challenge and give notice of anything passing down the river towards Northumberland and Sunbury. After the German Battalion left, it was garrisoned by the militia, when defended by any other than citizens. (In the History of the Forts, Penna. Archives, vol. xii, Appendix, p. 461, is "All we find about this fort is in a letter from Genl. Potter, dated Sunbury, September 18, 1780, in which he says I discharged the Volunteers that came from Cumberland and as soon as we could get provisions, which

was the next morning, I marched the remainder, consisting of
170 men, upon the West branch to Fort Swarts. I then went
to Col. Kelly, who lay at the mouth of White Deer creek with
80 men." On the 21st of September he again writes: "I gave
orders to the frontier companys to embody and keep one-
fourth of the men, constantly reconnoitering, after garrisoning
Fort Jenkins. Fort Rice and Fort Swarts, with 20 men in each
of them.") Day says Fort Swartz was one mile above Milton.
Meginness says at the ferry, about one mile above Milton, a
log structure garrisoned by and named for Major Christian
Godfried Swartz, of Col. Weltner's regiment.

FORT BRADY.

Fort Brady was the dwelling house of Capt. John Brady,
at Muncy, stockaded by digging a trench about four feet deep
and setting logs side by side, filling in with earth and ramming
down solid to hold the palisade in place. They were usually
twelve feet high from the ground, with smaller timbers running transversely at the top, to which they were pinned, making a solid wall. Capt. Brady's house was a large one for the
time; he had been a captain in the Scotch-Irish and German
forces west of the Alleghenies under Col. Henry Bouquet in
his expedition, which Dr. Egle tells us composed the Bouquet
expeditions, and had received a grant of land with the other
officers in payment for his services. He was a captain in the
12th Pennsylvania regiment in the Revolution and was wounded at the battle of the Brandywine. His son, John, a lad of
fifteen, stood in the ranks with a rifle and was also wounded.
Sam, his eldest son, was in another division and assisted to
make the record of Parr's and Morgan's riflemen world famous. The West Branch, in its great zeal for the cause of the
colonist, had almost denuded itself of fighting men for the
Continental army. Consequently, on the breaking out of Indian hostilities a cry for help went up from these sparsely
settled frontiers. Genl. Washington recognized the necessity
without the ability to relieve them. He, however, did all in

his power by mustering out such officers as would be likely to organize such defence and restore confidence to these justly alarmed communities, distributing the men among other regiments. Capt. John Brady was one of these officers; he was mustered out soon after the battle of Brandywine, came home and in the fall of 1777 stockaded Fort Brady. He was active, energetic, honest, devoid of fear and kind. A man of prominence and a natural leader of men. Fort Brady at once became a place of refuge to the families within reach in times of peril and continued so until after the death of the valiant captain and the driving off of the inhabitants. Capt. Brady was killed by the Indians at Wolf run, above Muncy, April 11, 1779. Meginness, in his History of the West Branch, says: "One of the saddest incidents of these troublesome times was the assassination of Capt. John Brady by a concealed foe on the 11th of April, 1779. He was living with his family at his fort, as it was termed, at Muncy, and was taking an active part against the Indians. On this fatal day he made a trip up the river to Wallis' for the purpose of procuring supplies. He took a wagon and guard with him, and, after securing a quantity of provisions started to return in the afternoon. He was riding a fine mare and was some distance in the rear of the wagon. Peter Smith, the same unfortunate man who lost his family in the bloody massacre of the 10th of June, and on whose farm young James Brady was mortally wounded and scalped by the Indians on the 8th of August, was walking by his side. When within a short distance of his home, Brady suggested to Smith the propriety of his taking a different route from the one the wagon had gone, as it was shorter. They traveled together until they came to a small stream of water (Wolf run), where the other road came in. Brady observed: This would be a good place for Indians to hide; Smith replied in the affirmative, when three rifles cracked and Brady fell from his horse dead. As his frightened mare was about to run past Smith he caught her by the bridle and, springing on her back, was carried to Brady's Fort in a few minutes. The report of the rifles was plainly heard at the fort and caused great alarm. Several persons rushed out, Mrs. Brady among them, and, seeing Smith coming at full speed, anxiously enquired where

Capt. Brady was. It is related that Smith, in a high state of excitement, replied: "In Heaven or hell, or on his way to Tioga," meaning he was either killed or a prisoner by the Indians. The Indians in their haste did not scalp him, nor plunder him of his gold watch, some money and his commission, which he carried in a green bag suspended from his neck. His body was brought to the fort and soon after interred in the Muncy burying ground, some four miles from the fort (now Hall's station, P. & E. R. R.) over Muncy creek." His grave is suitably marked at Hall's, while a cenotaph in the present Muncy cemetery of thirty feet high, raised by J. M. M. Gernerd by dollar subscription, attests the lively interest still felt by the community in one who devoted himself to the protection of the valley when brave active men and good counselors were needed. Of his sons, Capt. Samuel Brady, a sharpshooter of Parr's and Morgan's rifles, fought on almost every battlefield of the Revolution, from Boston and Saratoga to Germantown, can speak of his deeds as a scout and Indian fighter Western and Northern Pennsylvania, which West Virginia and Ohio attest. To the Indian he became a terror, and he fully avenged the blood of his sire shed at Wolf run, on the West Branch of the Susquehanna, that beautiful day in April, 1779, at the bloody fight of Brady's Bend, on the Allegheny, where, with his own hand, he slew his father's murderer and avenged his brother James, the "Young Captain of the Susquehanna," in a hundred other fights. Of his second son, James, killed by the Indians at the Loyal Sock, whose career bid fair to be as brilliant as his elder brother's but unfortunately cut off at his commencement. John, who, when but a boy of fifteen, going with his father and oldest brother to the battlefield of the Brandywine to bring back the horses, finding a battle on hand, took a rifle and stepped into the ranks and did manful duty, and was wounded. He is said to have served with Jackson at New Orleans in the War of 1812. William Perry Brady served on the northern borders in the same war, and at Perry's victory at Lake Erie, when volunteers were called, was the first to step out.

Hon. John Blair Linn, at the dedication of the Brady monument in 1879, one hundred years after the death of John
3*

Brady, said: "To the valley his loss was well nigh irrepar-
able; death came to its defender, and 'Hell followed' hard
after. In May, Buffalo Valley was overrun and the people
left, on the 8th of July Smith's mills, at the mouth of the
White Deer Creek were burned, and on the 17th Muncy valley
was swept with the besom of destruction. Starrett's mills and
all the principal houses in Muncy township burned, with
Fort Muncy, Brady and Freeland, and Sunbury became the
frontier."

And, in speaking of the fall of Capt. Evan Rice Brady at
South Mountain, in the war of '62, said: "Four generations of
the Bradys fought for this country, yet he was the first to fall
in action." The site of Fort Brady adjoins the town of Muncy,
on the south side of and near the built up portions of the town
on lot owned by Mrs. Hayes. Until late years, a flag staff has
stood, marking the site. Mr. J. M. M. Gernerd, the well-
known antiquarian of Muncy, keeps a good lookout for the
site. No question as to its genuineness.

FORT MUNCY.

Fort Muncy is located about half a mile above Hall's station, immediately on the P. & E. R. R., and about four miles
from Muncy, and was built by Col. Thomas Hartley in 1778, at
the urgent solicitation of Samuel Wallis, Esq., who had
erected a stone mansion here in 1769. It stood a few hundred yards in front of the famous Hall's house of 1769. It
was designed to be the most important stronghold next to Augusta, and was situated midway between that place and the
farthest settlement up the river; it was a rising piece of
ground at the foot of which was a fine spring of water, a large
elm tree now hangs over the spring. A covered way led from
the fort to this natural fountain as a protection to those who
went there for water. When the extension of the Philadelphia and Reading railroad was built to Williamsport, the ele
vation on which the fort stood was cut through. The excava
tion is quite deep and passengers cannot fail to notice it on ac

count of the view of the Hall residence on the left being suddenly shut off as the train dashes into the cut (in going up). Col. Hartley informs us that the bastions of the fort were built of fascines and clay and the curtains were protected by the stockades in which quarters for the garrison were placed. —(Maginness' Otzinachson, pages 484-5.)

One would understand from the many accounts that Fort Muncy had been destroyed twice. In the Penna. Archives, (Vol. xii, appendix, p. 418.) "The convoy arrived safely at Sunbury, leaving the entire line of farms along the West branch to the ravages of the Indians. They destroyed Fort Muncy, but did not penetrate Sunbury." Shortly after the big runaway Col. Brodhead was ordered up with his force of 100 or 150 men to rebuild Fort Muncy and guard the settlers while gathering their crops. After performing this service he left for Fort Pitt and Colonel Hartley, with a battalion succeeded him in 1778. Col. Ludwig Weltner, December 13th, 1779. I found Fort Muncy and Fort Jenkins, on the East branch, and with the magazine at Sunbury, to have been the only posts that were standing when he was ordered here from Wyoming.

"Col. Hunter, whom I consulted, was of the same opinion, the only difficulty was to fix on some place equally well adapted to cover the Frontier, as Fort Muncy was; Fort Muncy having been evacuated and destroyed." So Fort Muncy appears to have been destroyed the second time, as Lieut. Moses Van Campen, of Capt. Robinson's Rangers says, in the latter part of March, just at the opening of the campaign of 1782, the companies that had been stationed during the winter at Reading were ordered back by Congress to their respective stations; Lieut. Van Campen marched at the head of Capt. Robinson's company to Northumberland, where he was joined by Mr. Thomas Chambers, who had been recently commissioned ensign of the same company. Here he halted for a few days to allow his men rest, after which he was directed to march to a place called Muncy, and there rebuild a fort which had been destroyed by the Indians in the year '79. Having reached his station, he threw up a small blockhouse in which he placed his stores and immediately commenced rebuilding the fort, being joined shortly after by Capt. Robinson in company with several gentle-

men, among whom was a Mr. Culbertson, who was anxious to find
an escort up the West Branch of the Susquehanna into the
neighborhood of Bald Eagle creek. Here his brother had been
killed by the Indians, and being informed that some of his
party had been buried and had thus escaped the violence of
the enemy, he was desirous of making search to obtain it. Ar-
rangements were made for Van Campen to go with him at the
head of a small party of men as a guard. Lieut. Van Campen
was captured while on this expedition and taken to Canada,
where he remained some time, so we get no further information from him in regard to this rebuilding of Fort Muncy for
the third time. Fort Muncy, if properly garrisoned, was an
important position for the defense of the valley below it; here
was a good place from which to support scouting parties, west
and north, and from which passes of the Muncy hills to the
eastward could be covered by strong scouting parties, but the
country lacked men, and means to support them at this critical time. Near the site of Fort Muncy is the Indian Mound
described by Mr. Gernerd in his "Now and Then," and near the
Hall's station is the grave of Capt. John Brady, with his faith-
ful old soldier comrade, John Lebo, buried by his side. The
spring still defines the location of the fort.

FORT MENNINGER.

Fort Menninger was erected at White Deer Mills, or at the
time of building the Widow Smith's mills; it was built about
eighty rods from the river, on the north bank of White Deer
creek, covering the Widow Smith's mills, to which a gun barrel
boring establishment was added in 1776, and is said to
have turned out a good many of that much needed article.
The fort was situated west of the mills forming the apex of an
irregular triangle of which the mills formed one base and the
small stone house, said to have been erected by the Widow
Smith before the Revolution, which is not doubted, the other;
its walls are two feet thick, and the building is in good condition, having a more modern addition to it at present. The

fort and mills were abandoned at the time of the Big Runaway
in 1779, and the fort burned by the Indians July 8, 1779. In
John B. Linn's Annals of Buffalo Valley, pp. 239 and 240, we
find: "In a petition to the Assembly of this year, 1785, by
Catharine Smith, sets forth that she was left a widow with
ten children with no estate to support this family except a location for three hundred acres of land, including the mouth of
White Deer creek, whereon is a good mill seat, and a grist mill
and saw mill being much wanted in this new country at that
time, she was often solicited to erect said mills, which were of
great advantage to the country, and the following summer
built a boring mill, where a great number of gun barrels were
bored for the continent, and a hemp mill. The Indian war
soon after coming on, one of her sons, her greatest help, went
into the army and, it is believed, was killed, as he never returned. The said mills soon became a frontier and, in July,
1779, the Indians burned the whole works. She returned to
the ruins in 1783, and was again solicited to rebuild the grist
and saw mills, which she has, with much difficulty, accom-
plished, and now ejectments are brought against her by
Messrs. Claypool and Morris, and she, being now reduced to
such low circumstances as renders her unable to support ac-
tions at law, and therefore, prays relief, &c. The Legislature,
of course, could grant no relief under the circumstances and
the petition was dismissed." She is said to have gone to Philadelphia and back thirteen times on this business. Her house
was where Doctor Danonsky now (1874) lives, on the Henry
High place, part of the old stone house being used as a kitchen. Rolly McCorley, who recollects the mill last built by
her, said it was a small round log mill." A part of the foundation of this mill serves the same purpose in the fine modern mill
of to-day owned by Captain David Bly, of Williamsport, who
was born here and pointed out where, when a boy, he saw the
remains of Fort Menninger removed from. Fort Menninger
was built in the spring of 1778. Troops were stationed here a
part of the time after its destruction. In November, 1779,
fourteen men were stationed here, and most probably occupied
the Widow Smith's stone house.

Gen. James Potter (In Penna. Archives, Vol. viii. p.562), under

46

THE FRONTIER FORTS BETWEEN

date of Sept. 18, 1780, says: "I marched the remainder, consisting of 170 men up the West Branch to Fort Swarts. I then went to Col. Kelly, who lay at the mouth of White Deer creek, with 80 men."

FORT ANTES.

Fort Antes was erected by Lieut. Col. Henry Antes in 1778, about opposite Jersey Shore on the east side of Nippenose creek, and on the higher plateau overlooking it, and also the river. It was defended by Col. Antes, its builder, until ordered to vacate it by Col. Samuel Hunter, at the time the military authorities considered it unsafe to attempt to defend these forts.

Col. Hunter sent word to Col. Hepburn, then commanding at Fort Muncy to order all above him on the river to abandon the country and retire below. Meginness' Otizinachson says, "Col. Hepburn had some difficulty in getting a messenger to carry the order up to Col. Antes, so panic stricken were the people on account of the ravages of the Indians. At length, Robert Covenhoven and a young millwright in the employ of Andrew Culbertson, volunteered their services and started on the dangerous mission. They crossed the river and ascended Bald Eagle mountain and kept along the summit till they came to the gap opposite Antes' Fort. They then cautiously descended at the head of Nippenose Bottom and proceeded to the fort. It was in the evening and as they neared the fort the report of a rifle rang out upon their ears. A girl had gone outside to milk a cow, and an Indian lying in ambush fired upon her. The ball, fortunately, passed through her clothes and she escaped unhurt. The orders were passed on up to Horn's Fort and preparations made for the flight."

Fort Antes was a refuge for the Indian land or Fair Play men, as well as for those on the south side of the river. Col. Antes was a man of prominence in Northumberland county, in civil as well as military life. He was a justice of the peace and twice sheriff of Northumberland county. He was buried in a small grave yard near the fort he defended ably and

abandoned with great reluctance at the command of his superior officer. Near Fort Antes we were shown the scalping
knife, old flint lock pistol and pocket compass of the famous scout, guide and Indian fighter of the West Branch,
Robert Covenhoven. The knife has nine notches filed in the
back, to represent the number of Indians it has scalped.

Meginness says, "The most important defensive work, after
leaving Fort Muncy and traveling westward by the river
about twenty-five miles was what was known among the early
settlers at Antes' Fort, because it was built by Col. John
Henry Antes. It was located on a high bluff overlooking the
river and Indian land to the west, at the head of Long Island,
in what is now Nippenose township, Lycoming county. Although every trace of the fort has long since disappeared,
and the ground on which it stood is plowed and cultivated
annually, its name is perpetuated by the little village and
station on the Philadelphia and Erie railroad, about a mile
eastward, called Antes Fort."

The builder of this stockade, which played an important
part during the Indian troubles preceding the Big Runaway,
was one of the earliest pioneers to effect a permanent settlement here. It is believed that he was induced to locate lands
and settle here by Conrad Weiser, and that he came as early
as 1772. He picked out a mill site near the mouth of the creek
which still bears his name, erected a primitive dwelling place
and settled. At that time the surroundings must have been
exceedingly wild. The creek, which is the outlet for the
waters of Nippenose Valley, flows through a canon in the Bald
Eagle mountain which, at this day, possesses much of its native wilderness. Behind him rose the mountain, covered from
base to summit with its dark evergreen foliage of pine and
hemlock, whilst a swamp, with almost impenetrable thickets
of briars, tangled vines and underbrush, came up to within a
few yards of where he built his cabin.

Perhaps as early as 1773 he commenced the erection of a
grist mill. It was the most advanced improvement of its kind
up the river, and proved a great boon to the settlers for miles
beyond. To show the straightened circumstances of the inhabitants it may be mentioned that while the work of building

the mill was going on coarse flour was made by grinding wheat and corn in a large iron coffee mill, and the bran was removed by a hair sieve. Tradition says that one person was kept turning the mill all the time to keep a supply of flour for the sustenance of the workmen.

It cannot be positively stated when the stockade was built, but it must have been in the summer of 1777, when the Indians became demonstrative and troublesome on the frontier. The site selected for the fort was on the hill overlooking the mill, which was within rifle shot. It was constructed according to the usual plan, by sinking vertically heavy timbers in a trench dug four or five feet deep, when the earth was filled in around them.

These stockades were from ten to twelve feet high, and notched at the top for musketry. No record has been left to show the extent of the enclosure, but it must have covered fully a quarter of an acre, as a militia company was stationed there for several months. Whether the fort was ever supplied with small cannon or not is unknown, but a tradition has existed that it was, because a cannon ball was once found near the river bank, under the hill. It might have been carried there by some collector of Revolutionary relics. But as Fort Muncy had one or two, it is not improbable that one of these was dragged up to Antes' Fort to menace the savages when they appeared on the opposite side of the river.

Being active, vigilant and well informed for his time, John Henry Antes was appointed a justice of the peace for this part of Northumberland county on the 29th of July, 1775, by the court then held at Fort Augusta. He filled the office until the breaking out of Indian hostilities. On the 24th of January, 1776, he was appointed captain of a company of fifty-eight militiamen in the Second battalion under Col. James Potter, for the defence of the frontier, and he commanded a company in Col. William Plunket's regiment when he made his ill-timed raid on the Connecticut settlers at Wyoming.

After returning from the "raid" up the North Branch, he was commissioned a captain of foot in the Second battalion of Associators, April 19, 1776. In a little more than a year he was commissioned lieutenant colonel (May, 1777) of the Fourth battalion of the militia of Northumberland county, by the Supreme Executive Council, sitting at Philadelphia. His commission was beautifully written on parchment and signed by Thomas Wharton, Jr., president, and Timothy Matlack, secretary. It is still preserved by his descendants as a precious relic. On the 30th of July, 1777, he took the oath of allegiance and straightway entered on a more active career in the defence of the frontier against the savages, who were daily growing more bold and aggressive. It was about this time that he had a garrison at Antes' Fort and kept a vigilant outlook for the foe, who could come within sight of the fortification on their own land. Scouting parties were frequently sent out for the purpose of keeping communication open with Fort Muncy, and to watch the great Indian path running up Lycoming creek, down which scalping parties frequently came to ravage the settlements.

The winter of 1777-78 was rendered distressing by the frequent inroads of the savages, and it was necessary to observe the greatest vigilance to guard against surprise. On the 23d of December a man was tomahawked and scalped near the mouth of Pine creek, almost within sight of the fort; and of the 1st of January another met the same fate further up the river. This month Colonel Antes visited Fort Augusta to consult with Colonel Hunter as to what had best be done. The result of the conference was that three classes of Col. Cookson Long's battalion were ordered to report to Colonel Antes. The men composing these commands mostly lived on the West Branch and were good riflemen. The inhabitants, in view of the increasing danger, did not deem it prudent to allow any more militia to leave the country to join Washington's army, and so informed Colonel Hunter.

The scarcity of arms and ammunition was another drawback to a vigorous defence. Colonel Hunter was constantly clamoring for arms, but the authorities were so hard pressed that they could not meet his demands. The British were making a supreme effort both in the front and rear of Washington. Indians and Tories were directed to descend on the frontiers of Northumberland county, from Fort Niagara to destroy the settlements and show no mercy to men, women and children.

4

Colonel Antes had command of the frontier forces, with head-quarters at his stockade, and ranging parties were kept constantly in the field. Colonel Hunter stated that Colonel Antes was the only field officer he was allowed, and he found it almost impossible to defend the extensive frontier with the small force at his command.

A body of Indians numbering eleven were discovered skulking in the woods above the Great Island, and as it was evident that they were bent on mischief, they were promptly pursued by a portion of Colonel Antes' command. As a light snow had fallen they were easily tracked and soon overtaken. A slight skirmish ensued, when two Indians were killed. This caused the remaining nine to quickly take to the woods and escape. But, notwithstanding the vigilance of the scouting parties, small bands of Indians would suddenly appear in unlooked for places and do much damage.

The inhabitants complained that if no militia were stationed above Fort Muncy they would be forced to abandon their homes. This made it more responsible for Colonel Antes, and he was kept on the alert night and day. His stockade fort was the centre of military operations for months, and its value as a defensive point cannot be overestimated in those perilous times.

In June, 1777, an exciting and tragic affair occurred within sight of Fort Antes, which shows the constant danger to which the occupants were subjected. It was on a Sunday morning, when four men, Zephaniah Miller, Abel Cady, James Armstrong and Isaac Bouser, accompanied by two women, left the fort and crossed the river in canoes to the Indian land for the purpose of milking several cows which were pasturing there. The four men went along as a guard. One of the cows wore a bell but they found that she was further back from the shore than the others. Cady, Armstrong and Miller thoughtlessly started to drive her in to be milked. It never occurred to them that Indians might be lurking in the bushes and that the cow might be kept back as a decoy. Soon after entering the bushes they were fired upon by the concealed foe, and Miller and Cady fell, severely wounded. With the agility of cats they were pounced upon by the Indians and scalped, when they as quickly disappeared in the thickets. Armstrong was wounded in the back of the head, but succeeded in getting away. When the shots were fired, Bouser and the women, who were in the rear, ran to the river bank and concealed themselves.

The sudden firing alarmed the garrison at the fort, but a number of militiamen, friends of the party attacked, seized their guns and hurried across the river. Colonel Antes stoutly remonstrated against their going, fearing that it might be a decoy to draw the force away, when the fort would be assailed from the rear, but the men were so anxious to get a shot at the skulking savages that they could not be restrained, although aware that it was a breach of military discipline.

When the rescuing party reached the shore they soon found Cady and Miller where they fell, scalped, weltering in their blood, and presenting a horrible spectacle. Cady was still breathing, but unable to speak. He was picked up and carried to the river bank, where his wife, who was one of the milking party, met him. He reached out his hand to her as a sign of recognition and almost immediately expired. Armstrong was taken to the fort, where he lingered in great agony till Monday night following, when he died.

The loss of these three men, through the wily methods of the savages, caused a feeling of sadness among those collected in the fort, and showed them very plainly that their safety depended on vigilance. The pursuing party moved swiftly and soon came in sight of the Indians who, on seeing that they were discovered, turned and fired, but did no execution. They then dashed into a swamp which then existed under what is now the hill on which the Jersey Shore cemetery is situated. Deeming it unsafe to enter the tangled thickets of the swamp, the pursuing party returned. They fired several times at the retreating foe and thought they did some execution, as marks of blood were seen on their trail as if they had dragged away their killed or wounded.

One of the strange characters who was a frequent visitor to Antes Fort in those gloomy days was "Job Chilloway," a friendly Indian of the Delaware tribe. He had been converted by the Moravians and remained steadfast in the faith. Having associated much with the whites he became very friendly, and by many good acts won their confidence and respect. He was much employed as a scout by the military authorities and his fidelity was frequently proven by dangerous missions to gain information of the movement of the savages. He had a wide acquaintance among the Indians, as well as a thorough knowledge of the country, its mountains, streams and paths, and, therefore, was enabled to acquire information that proved of great value to the whites. At times he was suspected by the Indians of giving information, but through his artlessness and keenness of perception, he always managed to disabuse their minds of suspicion and escaped when others would have failed. In a word, he was a first class Indian detective, whose sense of gratitude never allowed him to prove recreant to his trust, and those who had befriended him, which was something remarkable in the nature and character of an aborigine. Through life he proved himself a "good Indian," and when he died near Fort Erie, Canada, September 22, 1792, he received Christian burial at the hands of his Moravian friends. He had learned to speak English well and understood several Indian dialects. He was the first to apprise the whites that the Indians were preparing to descend on the valley in force, and warned them to be prepared to resist the invaders.

Some interesting anecdotes illustrative of the character of this remarkable Indian, have been preserved, one of which may be related in this connection. One day, when the times were perilous, he was visiting at Antes Fort. As he was moving about outside the stockade, and ever on the alert for danger, he discovered a sentinel leaning against a tree asleep. Slipping up behind the tree he quickly threw his arms around it, and, grasping the sentinel, held him so that he could not see who had hold of him. The sentinel was badly frightened at his predicament and struggled to release himself, but in vain. At last he discovered that it was Job who had him pinioned, when he begged him not to tell Colonel Antes, who might punish him severely for such a grave offense. Job promised not to report him, but reminded him that if it had been an enemy that seized him, he might have been killed. "Yes," replied the sentinel, "I might have been caught by an Indian and killed before I knew who my assailant was." "It was an Indian that caught you," replied Job, with a grin, "but he was your friend."

This affair so much amused Job that he would burst into a fit of laughter whenever he thought of it. His frequent outbursts of merriment finally attracted the attention of Colonel Antes, and he asked what was the cause of it, but he refused to tell for a long time. At last he informed the Colonel that something serious had happened to one of his men, but he had pledged his word not to tell on him. But Job intimated to the Colonel that he might detect the guilty man by his countenance when the company was on parade. The Colonel scrutinized the countenance of his men sharply when they were paraded, which caused the guilty man to confess what occurred to him. The circumstance and the manner of its revealment through the suggestion of the Indian, so amused him that he did not punish the man, but admonished him not to be caught that way again.

In the early summer of 1778 another affair of an entirely different character occurred at the fort, which shows the prowling nature of the savages and how close they would venture to get a shot at a white person and possibly secure a scalp.

When Colonel Hunter sent word to the commanding officer at Fort Muncy that it would be necessary for the inhabitants living above the Muncy hills to abandon their homes and rendezvous at Fort Augusta, if they valued their lives, and despatched messengers with the warning to Antes Fort and Horn's Fort, some trouble was experienced in finding messengers who were willing to take the risk of traveling twenty-five miles up the valley, which was then infested by savages. Finally, Robert Covenhoven, the daring scout, and a young man employed at Culbertson's mill, volunteered to undertake the dangerous mission. The name of the young man, unfortunately for the benefit of history, has not been preserved, but the probabilities are that he did not go, because Covenhoven preferred, when on a dangerous mission, to go alone. We are led to this conclusion by the statement that Covenhoven started at once and stayed that night with a man named Andrew Armstrong, who had settled at a big spring a short distance east of the

present village of Linden. This was about sixteen miles west
of Fort Muncy and, therefore, a good stage for the first part
of the journey. It is of record that he warned Armstrong of
the impending danger and advised him to leave. He refused,
and, in a few days afterwards, was taken prisoner, carried
into captivity and never heard of again.

The next day Covenhoven did not take the risk of traveling
up the valley to Antes Fort, but, crossing the river, ascended
Bald Eagle mountain, and traveled along the level plateau on
the summit. He knew that the Indians were not likely to be
found there, as they preferred lying in ambush along the path
in the valley to surprise incautious travelers. Then, again, he
could look down into the valley and discover signs of Indians,
if any were about. The only point of danger was in descending
to cross one or two canons which intervened before debouch-
ing near the fort. He made the journey successfully, and, in
the evening as he was cautiously creeping through the bushes
and when within a few hundred yards of the fort, he was
startled by the sharp report of a rifle.

His first impression was that he had been discovered and
fired upon by an Indian concealed in the bushes, but finding
himself uninjured he made a dash for the fort, which he
reached in safety and delivered the message of Colonel Hunter to Colonel Antes to evacuate the place within a week.

Investigation showed that the shot had been fired by an Indian at a young woman who had gone outside the fort to milk
a cow. The Indian had stealthily crawled up until he got in
range and fired. The young woman was badly frightened, as
she had made a narrow escape. The bullet passed through the
folds of her dress without touching her person. Milking cows
in those days outside of a fort was a dangerous experiment,
and several narrow escapes are recorded.

As soon as the shot was fired a body of armed men rushed
out of the fort and scoured the surrounding neighborhood for
some distance, but the venturesome redskin could not be
found. He had probably taken refuge in the swamp, about a
quarter of a mile southwest of the fort—a favorite hiding
place with the Indians.

It does not appear that Covenhoven continued to Horn's fort

—another messenger evidently having conveyed the news there—as we are informed that he immediately returned to Fort Muncy. The brief record of the times does not tell us how he returned, but as an Indian lurked in nearly every thicket, we are left to infer that he made his way back by the mountain route, as it was the safest. In a few days afterwards we hear of him removing his wife to Fort Augusta for safety, and then returning to assist the panic stricken inhabitants in their flight down the river in what was known as the Big Runaway.

In less than a month after the flight armed bodies of men were hurried up the valley from Fort Augusta and posted at Fort Muncy, whence scouting parties were sent out to see what damage had been done. They found the cabins and barns of the settlers burned and their crops greatly damaged. In about a month many settlers were induced to return and gather what they could of their crops under the protection of armed men.

An advance scouting party hurried up the river as far as Antes Fort. They found the mill and outbuildings burned and the embers yet smoking, showing that the savages had just been there before them. The air was tainted with the aroma of roasting wheat, and everything destructible attested the work of the vandals. Antes Fort, however, was still tenable; the savages were unable to burn the stout oaken timbers which formed the stockade, and they were not disposed to undertake the hard labor of cutting them down or pulling them out of the earth, where they had been so firmly implanted. Everything else that could be destroyed was rendered useless.

Colonel Antes and family fled with the rest of the fugitives in obedience to the orders of Colonel Hunter, but he was among the first to return to look after his property. It does not appear that any militia were stationed at the fort again for any length of time, although it is probable that it was made a rallying point until all danger was over. On the restoration of peace it was allowed to fall into decay, and it soon became a ruin, which for many years was pointed out by the old settlers as a spot of great historic interest, on account of its association with the thrilling days of the Revolutionary period.

Colonel Antes, soon after the return of peace rebuilt his mill and for years it was the only one in that section of the valley to supply the settlers with flour, who came with their grists as far away as thirty or forty miles, and in some instances further. A mill still stands on the site to-day, although it is the third since the first.

This remarkable man, who played such a conspicuous part in the early history of the valley in both a military and civil capacity, was born October 8, 1736, near Pottstown, Montgomery county. His ancestors came from Crefeld on the Rhine, and in this country they occupied high positions in the Dutch Reformed church. His parents had eleven children, all of whom were ardent patriots and the males were distinguished for their military services in Revolutionary times.

Colonel Antes was chosen sheriff of Northumberland county in 1782, and commissioned on the 18th of October. He was re-elected in 1783, and served a second term. His first wife—Anna Maria Paulin—died in March, 1767, leaving five children. By his second wife, Sophia Snyder, he had eight children. Colonel Antes had an elder brother, Philip Frederick, who married Barbara Tyson in 1755. Their youngest daughter, Catharine, married Simon Snyder about 1796. He became Governor of Pennsylvania in 1808, and served until 1817—three terms.

The Colonel was an active and busy man. He acquired considerable land on Antes creek and made many improvements. He died May 13, 1820, aged 83 years, 9 months and 5 days, and was buried in the graveyard near his famous fortification. This burial ground was started by those who were killed by the Indians. Here Donaldson (see sketch of Horn's Fort), McMichael and Fleming were buried, and here Cady, Miller and Armstrong were laid at rest. Since that time—one hundred and seventeen years ago—scores of old and young have found a place of sepulture in its sacred soil, and burials are still made there.

No stone marks the grave of the old hero and patriot, Col. John Henry Antes, although the spot is pointed out by some of his descendants where he was laid three-quarters of a century ago. Considering what he did in a military capacity alone, the trials he passed through, the hardships he endured and the foundation he assisted in laying for the higher civilization which followed him, the time has arrived for the erection of a suitable monument to perpetuate his name and fame. Marble, granite, brass and bronze testimonials have been reared over the graves of those who did less for posterity; here lies one who is eminently deserving of an appropriate block of granite, indicative of his rugged character and sublime patriotism. Shall it be done or must his memory be allowed to perish?

.

FORT HORN.

Fort Horn was erected on a high flat extending out to the river and commanding a good view of the river up and down, as well as the north side of the river; is about midway between Pine and McElhattan Stations on the P. & E. R. R., west of Fort Antes. It was a place of refuge for those hardy settlers on the Indian lands on the north side of the river, as well as the residents on the Pennsylvania lands on which it was built. The river lands on the north side were outside the purchase of 1768, from the Lycoming creek up the river westward. These settlers were adventurous, hardy, brave. When I say they were mostly Scotch-Irish it will be understood they were also law abiding. As they were outside the limits of the laws of the Province, they had formed a code of their own and administered it impartially. In troublous times now upon these communities they all stood shoulder to shoulder, proving the saying that blood is thicker than water.

A few soldiers are said to have been stationed here and the settlers on both sides the river joined them in scouting duty, sending word to those below of approaching danger; several light skirmishes took place between the men of the fort and the Indians, in which several lives were lost. On an alarm, the inhabitants of the north side placed their families in canoes and paddled to Antes, Horn and Reid's forts; when danger passed over their families would return.

Accompanied by John F. Meginness, the historian, J. H. MacMinn, a great-grandson of Col. Antes, and quite an antiquarian, we visited the sites of these upper West Branch forts. A Mr. Quiggle, of Pine, accompanied us to Fort Horn. The old gentleman pointed out to us the depression where, in his younger days, had stood up the remains of the stockades. The P. & E. R. R. at this point has cut away about one-half the ground enclosed by the fort.

This stockaded fortification was situated on a commanding point of land on the West Branch of the Susquehanna river, in what is now the township of Wayne, Clinton county, one mile west of the post village of Pine. At this point the river describes a great bend, affording a commanding view for about one mile up and down the stream from the elevation or point on which Samuel Horn chose to erect his stockade. Looking across the river to the north, which, at this point flows to the east, a magnificent view of the rich, alluvial valley is afforded; in the rear, not more than one-fourth of a mile away, is the dark and sombre range of the Bald Eagle mountain, varying in altitude from five to seven hundred feet.

At the time Samuel Horn settled here the river was the Indian boundary line, according to the provisions of the treaty of 1768, therefore, he was on the northern boundary of the Province of Pennsylvania. From the point where he built his cabin he could look over the Indian possessions for miles and plainly see the cabins of a dozen or more sturdy Scotch Irish squatters on the "forbidden land." The tract on which Horn settled was warranted in the name of John L. Webster in 1769. Since that time it has passed through a number of hands, and is now owned by a Mr. Quiggle, whose ancestors were among the early settlers in this part of Wayne township.

Horn, when the Indians became threatening in 1777, with the assistance of his neighbors, enclosed his primitive log dwelling with stockades, and it became a rallying point as well as a haven of safety, in the perilous times which followed. The line of stockades can be pretty clearly traced to this day by the depression in the ground and the vegetation and underbrush. The enclosure probably embraced a quarter of an acre, thereby affording ample room for a number of families. A small stream of pure mountain water ran along the western side of the enclosure, and it is probable that there was a way constructed so that it could be reached from within with safety from the prowling foe. When the Philadelphia and Erie railroad was built the line cut through the northern end of what has been the stockaded enclosure, and the discolored earth showed very plainly where the timber had decayed.

Horn's Fort and the others of the upper West Branch were recognized by the authorities as defensive positions, and most of them, if not all, furnished with troops, either militia or Continental, when troops could be procured for that purpose; when not garrisoned by militia, these forts on this flank, were held by the inhabitants of the Province of the south side of the river, assisted by their neighbors of the Indian lands of the north side.

Colonel Antes was furnished militia to strengthen Antes Fort whenever Colonel Hunter, the commander of Northumberland county, could procure them. Moses Van Campen tells us Colonel Kelly's regiment of militia garrisoned Fort Reid, at now Lock Haven, a few miles above Horn's, the most of the summer of 1777.

Tradition says that Horn's was a defensive work of no mean importance at that time, and was of great value to the pioneers who had pushed their way up the river in the advance guard, as it were. There was but one defensive work (Reid's) a few miles west, and as it was on the extreme limits of the frontier there a company of county militia was stationed for some time. Its location was admirably chosen. In all that region no more eligible position could have been formed. Standing on its ramparts, the eye swept the river right and left and the Indian lands to the north, for several miles. As the current bore immediately under its lee, an Indian canoe could scarcely have glided past in the night without having been detected by a vigilant sentinel.

One of the most remarkable incidents of Revolutionary times—an incident which stands, so far as known, without its counterpart in the history of the struggle of any people for liberty and independence, occurred within sight of Horn's fort, but across the river on the Indian land. This was what is known as the "Pine Creek Declaration of Independence." The question of the colonies throwing off the yoke of Great Britain and setting up business for themselves, had been much discussed, both in and out of Congress. The hardy Scotch Irish settlers on both sides of the river, in the vicinity of Horns, bore little love for the mother country. The majority of them had been forced to leave their native land and to seek a home where they would be free from religious oppression—where they could worship God according to the dictates of their own conscience. They were all patriots in the broadest sense of the term, and a loyalist or tory would not have been tolerated in their midst. They yearned for independence, and when the discussion of the subject waxed warm they resolved on calling a public meeting to give formal expression to their views. Accordingly, on the 4th day of July, 1776, the meeting, assembled on the Pine creek plains and a resolution was passed, declaring themselves free and independent of Great Britain. The remarkable feature of this meeting was that the Pine creek resolution was passed on the same day that a similar resolution was passed by the Continental Congress sitting in Philadelphia, more than two hundred miles away, and between whom there could be no communication for concert of action. It was, indeed, a remarkable coincidence—remarkable in the fact that the Continental Congress and the squatter sovereigns on the West Branch should declare for freedom and independence about the same time.

It is regretted that no written record of the meeting was preserved, showing who the officers were and giving the names of all those present. All that is known is what has been handed down by tradition. The following names of the participants have been preserved: Thomas, Francis and John Clark, Alexander Donaldson, William Campbell, Alexander Hamilton, John Jackson, Adam Carson, Henry McCracken, Adam DeWitt, Robert Love and Hugh Nichols. The meeting might have been held at the cabins of either John Jackson or Alexander Hamilton, as both were representative and patriotic men of the period. Several of these men afterwards perished at the hands of the savages; others fought in the Revolutionary army and assisted in achieving the independence which they had resolved the country should have.

The majority of these men lived across the river from the fort on the Indian land, and they all received patents for the land they had pre-empted after the treaty and purchase of 1784, in consideration of their loyalty, patriotism and devotion to the struggling colonies. The name of Samuel Horn is not found among those that have been handed down to us, but it may be safely inferred that the man who was sufficiently patriotic to build a stockade fort for the protection of the neighborhood in which these men lived, was a sympathizer, if not a participant, in the Pine creek movement for independence.

There is nothing on record to show that the fort was ever supplied with small cannon. Its only armament was muskets and rifles in the hands of the hardy settlers when they had collected there in times of danger. That the savages regarded it with displeasure, and sought more than one opportunity to attack the occupants, there is abundant proof. They prowled about in small bands or laid concealed in the surrounding thickets ready to shoot down and scalp any thoughtless occupant who might venture a few hundred yards from the enclosure. Among the thrilling escapes that have been preserved is that of the young woman named Ann Carson, just before the flight known in history as the Big Runaway. She ventured out of the fort one day and was fired upon by a concealed savage. The bullet cut through the folds of her dress, making fourteen holes in its flight, but left her uninjured. About the same time another young woman named Jane Anesley, while engaged in milking a cow one evening outside the enclosure, was fired at by a lurking Indian several times. One bullet passed through her dress, grazing her body so closely that she felt the stinging sensation so severely that she was sure she was shot.

At the time Colonel Hunter sent up word from Fort Augusta for the settlers to abandon the valley and flee to places of safety down the river, as he was informed that a large body of savages was preparing to descend from the Seneca country to devastate the valley and wipe out the settlements, that fear-

less scout and intrepid soldier, Robert Covenhoven, bore the
unwelcome news from Fort Muncy to Antes Fort and had a
messenger dispatched from the latter place to warn the inmates of Fort Horn that they must fly if they valued their
lives. The meagre records informs us that all the settlers within a radius of several miles were collected at Horn's and that
a great state of excitement prevailed. Those living on the Indian lands across the river were gathered at the fort, anxiously
awaiting news from below. Judging from the extent of the
settlements at the time, a hundred or more fugitives must
have been collected there.

The order to evacuate the fort was received with feelings of
alarm, well nigh bordering on despair. The frenzied settlers
at once set about making preparations to abandon their
humble homes, their growing crops—for it was in early June—
and fly. Many of them buried chinaware and other household
effects that they could not well carry with them in places that
they could recognize if they were ever permitted to return.

Soon after receiving Colonel Hunter's message four men,
Robert Fleming, Robert Donaldson, James McMichael and
John Hamilton started down the river in canoes for Antes Fort
to secure a flat in which to transport their families below. They
were squatters on the Indian land across the river from Horn's
and they knew that the savages had a grudge against them for
trespassing on their territory, and that they would fare badly
if they fell in their hands. The dread of impending danger
had driven them across the river with their families to seek
the protection of the fort.

They reached Antes Fort in safety, engaged a flat and started
on their return. But the eye of the wily savage was on them.
They had pushed their canoes up through the Pine creek riffles,
when they pushed over to the south side of the river for the
purpose of resting and to await for other parties who were following them with the flat. At this point the mountain comes
down almost to the edge of the river, and at that time it presented an exceedingly wild and forbidding appearance. As
they were about to land, and not suspecting danger, they were
suddenly fired on by a small band of savages concealed in the
bushes. Donaldson jumped out of his canoe, rushed up the

bank and cried to the others, "Come on, boys." Hamilton saw
the Indians rise up, and at the same time noticed the blood
spurting from a wound in Donaldson's back as he was trying
to reload his gun. He soon fell from exhaustion and died. Fleming
and McMichael were also killed. Hamilton, who was un-
touched, gave his canoe a powerful shove into the stream and,
jumping into the water fell flat on the other side. Then, holding the canoe with one hand between the Indians and himself,
he managed to paddle across the river with the other. Several
bullets flew around his frail craft, but he escaped without a
scratch. When he landed his woolen clothes were so heavy,
from being saturated with water, as to impede his flight.
He, therefore, stripped himself of everything but his shirt and
ran swiftly up the river. His route was by the Indian path to
the Great Island. He ran for life. Fear lent wings to his
flight. The flutter of a bird stimulated him to increase his
speed, and if a bush came in his way he cleared it with a
bound. In this way he ran for nearly three miles, passing the
place where his father had settled, until he came opposite
Horn's fort, when he was discovered and a canoe was sent to
rescue him.

The men in the flat being behind and hearing the firing and,
divining the cause, hurriedly pushed to the north shore, below
the mouth of Pine creek, which they hurriedly forded and ran
up the path which Hamilton had so swiftly traveled. James
Jackson, who was one of the party on the flat, found a horse
pasturing on the Pine creek clearing which he caught,
mounted and rode up to the point opposite Horn's fort, when
he was discovered and brought over in a canoe. The other
men made their way to the fort and escaped.

An armed body of men, as soon as the news was received at
Horn's, made their way down to the place of ambuscade. Here
the dead and scalped bodies of Donaldson, McMichael and
Fleming were found, but the Indians had departed. They
knew that they would be punished and hurried away as
quickly as possible. The rescuing party secured the three
dead bodies of their neighbors and carried them to Antes Fort,
where they were buried in the little graveyard which had been
started outside of the enclosure. Nearly all of these men left

families, and the cruel manner in which they had been slain caused great excitement at the fort, as well as intense grief on the part of their wives and children. It was a sad day at Horn's. But no time was to be lost. Activity was the demand of the hour. The savages were emerging from the forests on every hand bent on murder and pillage, and the settlers collected at the fort saw that if they were to escape their relentless fury they must fly at once.

The same day the bloody affair occurred at Pine creek, a party of men were driving a lot of cattle down the river from the vicinity of the Great Island—the thickest part of the settlement on the Indian land—when they were fired on by a small body of skulking savages, almost in sight of Fort Horn. The whites, who were well armed, returned the fire, when an Indian was observed to fall and was quickly removed by his companions. This mishap seemed to strike terror into the ranks of the survivors and they fled precipitately into the forest, abandoning a lot of plunder, consisting largely of blankets, which fell into the hands of the whites. A member of the cattle party named Samuel Fleming, was shot through the shoulder and severely wounded. The Fleming family was one of the earliest to settle in this neighborhood, and as the head thereof had several sons, it is probable that Samuel was a brother of Robert, who was killed in the ambuscade at Pine Creek.

The firing was heard at Horn's and added to the alarm of the women and children assembled there, which only subsided when they found the party approaching on the other side of the river with their cattle. Fleming was ferried over to the fort, where he had his wound dressed. The cattle drivers continued on down the river in search of a place of greater security for their stock.

Such were some of the incidents preceding the Big Runaway in the latter part of June, 1778, when all of that part of the valley of the West Branch, west of the Muncy hills, was abandoned by the white settlers to escape the fury of the savages. The stockade forts, like the humble log cabins, were dismantled and burned, so far as the remorseless foe was capable of carrying out their intentions.

A description of the Big Runaway, which has no parallel

in frontier history, is not out of place in this connection.   The best account is found in Sherman Day's Historical Collections of Pennsylvania, p. 451.   Mr. Day obtained it from the lips of Covenhoven himself in 1842, more than fifty years ago, when the thrilling incidents were comparatively fresh in his mind. After delivering the order of Colonel Hunter to the commander of Antes Fort, and seeing that the message was conveyed to Horn's, Covenhoven hastily returned to Fort Muncy and removed his wife to Sunbury for safety.   He then started up the river in a keel boat for the purpose of securing his scanty household furniture and to aid the panic stricken inhabitants to escape.   Day reports his story in these thrilling words:

"As he was rounding a point above Derrstown (now Lewisburg) he met the whole convoy from all the forts above (Muncy, Antes, Horn's and Reid's) and such a sight he never saw in his life.   Boats, canoes, hog troughs, rafts hastily made of dry sticks—every sort of floating article had been put in requisition and were crowded with women and children and 'plunder'—there were several hundred people in all.   Whenever any obstruction occurred at a shoal or riffle, the women would leap out and put their shoulders, not, indeed, to the wheel, but to the flat boat or raft, and launch it again into deep water.   The men of the settlement came down in single file on each side of the river to guard the women and children. The whole convoy arrived safely at Sunbury, leaving the entire line of farms along the West Branch to the ravages of the Indians.   They did not penetrate in any force near Sunbury, their attention having been soon after diverted to the memorable descent on Wyoming.   *   *   *   After Covenhoven had got his bedding and furniture in his boat (at Loyalsock, and was proceeding down the river just below Fort Meuninger (at the mouth of White Deer creek), he saw a woman on the shore fleeing from an Indian.   She jumped down the river bank and fell, perhaps, wounded by his gun.   The Indian scalped her, but in his haste neglected to tomahawk her.   She survived the scalping, was picked up by the men from the fort (Freeland) and lived on Warrior run until about the year 1840.   Her name was Mrs. Durham."

5

Strange as it may seem, nothing has been preserved to show who Samuel Horn was, whence he came or whither he went after abandoning his fort. Neither do the records show that he ever warranted any land in that vicinity. That he had a family is reasonably certain, else it is not likely he would have gone to the trouble and expense of building a stockade around his cabin for protection and the protection of his neighbors, who made it a rallying point in time of great danger. All that has been preserved about him is what has been handed down in the form of tradition. It is probable that he never returned after the Big Runaway, but settled in some of the lower counties. His name, however, has been perpetuated in connection with the fort, and, although one hundred and sixteen years have rolled away since he hurriedly bade it adieu forever, the site where it stood is still proudly pointed out by the people in the neighborhood, who hold his name in grateful remembrance.

This report would be incomplete if no further reference was made to the fearless scout—Robert Covenhoven—who bore the last message up the river warning the settlers to fly to Fort Augusta to escape the wrath of the red-handed Ishmaelites who were bearing down on them from the north incited to commit the most atrocious deeds by the promise of British gold.

Who was Robert Covenhoven? He was of Hollandish descent, and came with his father's family from Monmouth county, New Jersey, where he was born December 7, 1755, and settled near the mouth of Loyalsock creek in 1772. A number of relatives accompanied them. Our subject—the name has since been corrupted in Crownover—was first employed as a hunter and axeman by the surveyors, and early became acquainted with the paths of the wilderness and inured to the dangers and hardships of pioneer life. This knowledge and service eminently fitted him to perform the duties of a scout, and as he was fearless, strong and sagacious and well acquainted with the wiles of the Indian, he became very successful in his dangerous calling.

On the breaking out of the Revolution he joined Washington's army and participated in the battles of Trenton and

Princeton. In the spring of 1777 he was sent to his home on the West Branch to aid in protecting the frontiers, and few men in those stirring times endured greater hardships or had more hairbreadth escapes. He married Miss Mercy Kelsey Cutter (also a native of New Jersey), February 22, 1778, so that it will be seen that she was little more than a bride at the time of the Big Runaway.

To give a history of his life in full would require the space of a moderate sized volume. He was the principal guide for Colonel Hartley when he made his famous expedition up Lycoming creek in September, 1778, by direction of Congress for the purpose of chastising the Indians at Tioga Point (now Athens), and was the first man to apply the torch to the wigwam of Queen Esther at the Point.

He had a brother killed in a fight with Indians on Loyalsock, near where his father settled, and had another taken prisoner. He was himself chased for some distance along the creek, dodging up and down the bank alternately, that his savage pursuers might get no aim at him. Doubtless, his swiftness of foot and power of endurance saved him. He escaped to Fort Muncy and gave an account of the fight. On the close of the war he purchased a farm in Level Corner, Lycoming county, almost in sight of Antes Fort, and settled down to the quiet pursuits of agriculture.

He had a family of five sons and three daughters, all of whom are deceased. His wife died November 27, 1843, aged 88 years, 10 months and 8 days, and was buried in a cemetery on what is now West Fourth street, Williamsport. Her grave has been obliterated by a church, which stands on the spot where it was made.

When the veteran grew old and was borne down by the weight of years, he went to stay with a daughter who lived near Northumberland. There he died October 29, 1846, at the ripe and mellow age of 90 years, 10 months and 22 days, and was laid at rest in the old Presbyterian graveyard in the borough of Northumberland. A plain marble headstone marks his grave, and the inscription, now almost illegible, tells who he was and what he did to help achieve our independence. For years the old burial ground where his ashes repose has been a common, and cattle graze on its green sward in summer time, pigs root among fallen tombstones and listless vandals amuse themselves by defacing memorial tablets reared by loving hands to perpetuate the name of a father or mother. The old patriot left a request in his will to be buried by the side of his wife, but his executor failed to carry it out, and from appearances his humble grave will soon be obliterated, the corroding tooth of time will soon destroy his plain marble tablet, and his numerous descendants will no longer be able to tell where his bones were laid.

FORT REID AT LOCK HAVEN.

Fort Reid was the most westerly of the line of defences thrown out in advance of Fort Augusta, for the purpose of covering that place and as a rallying place for the inhabitants and the scouts when hard pressed. The Continental army had drawn largely upon the young active men of the region, leaving those less fit for active service at home to cope with an enemy, the most active and wily in border warfare of this kind in the world.

In this forest country, with the inhabitants isolated by the size of their land claims, he could lay in wait, concealed for weeks if necessary, to await an opportunity to strike the settler when off his guard or in a situation in which he could offer least effective opposition. Not hampered with baggage, never troubled about keeping open his communications, as he could glide through where a fox might pass, and as noiselessly: armed by his master with the best of arms the time afforded, while the pioneers could scarcely procure ammunition enough to keep his family in meat; the Indian was bountifully furnished from the ample storehouses of the English. One naturally wonders how, with all the disadvantages against him, the settler held out so long; his staying qualities were wonderful; with these strengthened houses inadequately garrisoned as the only refuge for his family, he was a man who elicits our admiration.

Reid's Fort was the dwelling house of Mr. William Reid, stockaded in the spring of 1777; its location is on Water or River street, in the built up part of the town east of the mouth of the Bald Eagle canal. Judge Mayer and others have kept up an interest in its site. Visiting the site, Capt. R. S. Barker and myself called upon William Quigley and his wife, who were said to be the oldest residents of the place, he being ninety years; we found the pair bright, intelligent people. He recollected the remains of Fort Reid and so did Mrs. Quigley. As their location is acquiesced in by Judge Mayer and the others, we give it.

A large Indian mound existed at this place on the river bank, described as high as a two-story house, surrounded by a circle of small ones. In digging the Bald Eagle canal they cut away the western half of this mound, exhuming quantities of human bones and stone implements. The banks of the canal were said to be whitened therewith for years after. Immediately to the east of the mounds and close thereto stood Reid's fort, traces of which could be seen after 1820. This gives us the exact site within, say thirty feet, of the chimney of the Reid house and brings us within the stockades.

As mentioned before it was the left flanking defence of the series and was vacated by order of Col. Hunter, who had command of these forts, and garrisoned when he had troops, but the principal defence fell upon the settlers of the regions they protected. The Indians seldom attacked these places with any persistency unless accompanied by whites. It was an important point to garrison, covering the river on both sides and the lower Bald Eagle valley, which, when well done by the assistance of Horn, Antes and Muncy, protected the whole of the region between the Bald Eagle and the Susquehanna down to White Deer creek.

Moses Van Campen, then orderly sergeant of Captain Gaskins' company of Colonel John Kelly's regiment of Northumberland county militia, says the regiment was stationed here at Fort Reid during its six months' service in the summer of 1777. As he calls it Fort Reid it must have been fortified at that time, as the position was on the extreme outer limits of the settlements and much exposed. This is, without doubt, correct. Scouting duty was performed by the regiment and guarding the inhabitants was performed vigilantly. Here, in the West Branch, is located at the mouth of the Bald Eagle creek, the "Big Island," comprising a few hundred acres and very fertile. This place attracted settlers early, while on each side of the river the lands were attractive and a considerable settlement existed in the vicinity of the fort at this time. Here Van Campen had his wrestling match with the champion of the Indian land men, or those settlers on the north side of the river, in which Northumberland's activity and muscle prevailed. Here the Bald Eagle valley terminates. The fort, when manned as it should be, protected the lower part of the valley. The Rev. Mr. Fithian, of the Presbyterian church, visited this place before the Revolution, going with Miss Jenny Reed and another young woman whortleberrying on the Bald Eagle mountain. On returning from the expedition they came part of the way by the river; their canoeman was unfortunate and overset the canoe, spilling out the girls and whortleberries. The water was not deep; the girls squalled lustily at first, but, finding themselves unhurt, they proceeded to chastise the canoeman by "skeeting" water over him with their tin cups until the poor fellow was effectually drenched, when, still indignant, they waded to the shore to their friends, who were there enjoying the scene.

The foregoing includes all the forts built as a defence against the Indians prior to 1783 I find in my jurisdiction, and they are fifteen in number.

BIBLIOGRAPHY

OF THE

WYOMING HISTORICAL AND GEOLOGICAL SOCIETY,

WILKESBARRÉ, PENNSYLVANIA.

WYOMING HISTORICAL AND GEOLOGICAL SOCIETY. Proceedings and Collections. Vols. 1–3. Wilkes-Barre, 1858–1886. Three vols., 8vo. pp. 315+294+128. $10.00.

CONTENTS.

—Vol. 1, No. 1. Mineral Coal. Two Lectures, by Volney L. Maxwell. 1858. pp. 52. Reprinted as follows: 2d edition, N. Y., 1858; 3d edition, with a preface, N. Y., 1860, pp. 52; 4th edition, with a preface, Wilkes-Barre, 1869, pp. 51. $1.00.

—Vol. 1, No. 2. Proceedings at the Annual Meeting, February 11, 1881; Minutes; Report of Treasurer; Report of Cabinet Committee; Report of Committee on Flood of 1865; "A Yankee Celebration at Wyoming in Ye Olden Time," an historical address, by Steuben Jenkins. 1881. pp. 58. Out of print.

—Vol. 1, No. 3. Proceedings for the Year ending February 11, 1882; List of Contributors; Communication of John II. Dager (of gauge readings at Wilkes-Barre bridge for 1880); Meteorological Observations for May, 1881–January, 1882, by E. L. Dana; Incidents in the Life of Capt. Samuel H. Walker, Texan Ranger, by Gen. E. L. Dana. 1881. pp. 58. $0.50.

—Vol. 1, No. 4. A Memorandum Description of the Finer Specimens of Indian Earthenware Pots in the collection of the Society. By Harrison Wright. 1883. pp. (10). Seven heliotype plates. $1.00.

—Vol. 1, No. 5. List of Palæozoic Fossil Insects of the United States and Canada, with references to the principal Bibliography of the Subject. Paper read April 6, 1883, by R. D. Lacoe. 1883. pp. 21. $0.50.

—Vol. 1, No. 6. Proceedings for the Year ending February 11, 1883; List of Contributors; Meteorological Observations, February, 1882–January, 1883, by Gen. E. L. Dana. pp. 70. $0.75.

—Vol. 1, No. 7. Isaac Smith Osterhout. Memorial. 1883. pp. 14. Portrait. $0.75.

—Vol. 1, No. 8. Ross Memorial. General William Sterling Ross and Ruth Tripp Ross. 1884. Two portraits. 1858–1884. 8vo., pp. 17. $1.00.

—Vol. 1. Title page. Contents. Index. pp. xi.

—Vol. 2, PART I. Charter; By-Laws; Roll of Membership; Proceedings, March, 1883–February, 1884; Meteorological Observations taken at Wilkes-Barre, March, 1883–January, 1884, by E. L. Dana; Report of the Special Archæological Committee on the Athens locality, by Harrison Wright; Local Shell Beds, by Sheldon Reynolds; Pittston Fort, by Steuben Jenkins; A Bibliography of the Wyoming Valley, by Rev. Horace Edwin Hayden; Calvin Wadhams, by Geo. B. Kulp. PART II. Proceedings, May 9, 1884–February 11, 1886; Archæological Report, by Sheldon Reynolds; Numismatical Report, by Rev. Horace Edwin Hayden; Palæontological Report, by R. D. Lacoe; Mineralogical Report, by Harrison Wright; Conchological Report, by Dr. Charles F. Ingham; Contributions to Library; Meteorological Observations taken at Wilkes-Barre, February, 1884–January, 1885, by E. L. Dana; Rev. Bernard Page, by Sheldon Reynolds; Various Silver and Copper Medals presented to the American Indians by the Sovereigns of England, France and Spain, from 1600 to 1800, by Rev. H. E. Hayden; Report on some Fossils from the lower coal measures near Wilkes-Barre, by E. W. Claypole; Report on the Wyoming Valley Carboniferous Limestone Beds, by Charles A. Ashburner; Obituaries, by George B. Kulp. Index. 1886. pp. 294. Illustrated. $3.00.

—Vol. 3. In Memoriam. Harrison Wright, A. M., Ph. D.; Proceedings of the
· Society; Biographical Sketch, by G. B. Kulp; Literary Work, by Sheldon Reynolds, M. A.; Poem, by D. M. Jones; Luzerne County Bar proceedings; Trustees of Osterhout Free Library Resolutions; Historical Society of Pennsylvania, proceedings. 1886. 8vo., pp. 128. Portrait. $3.00.

Annals of Luzerne County. By Stewart Pearce. Philadelphia. 1860. 8vo. pp. 554. Folded map. Dedicated to the Society. Same, second edition, with notes, corrections and valuable additions. Philadelphia. 1860. 8vo. pp.. 564.

Sketch of the Society, by C. B. Johnson. Reprinted from the *Sunday News-Dealer*, Christmas edition. Wilkes-Barre. 1880. 8vo., pp. 7.

Report of a Committee of the Society on the early Shad Fisheries of the North Branch of the Susquehanna River, by Harrison Wright, Ph. D., chairman of the committee. In U. S. Fish Commission *Bulletin*. 1882. pp. 352–359. $1.00.

A Circular of Inquiry from the Society respecting the old Wilkes-Barre Academy. Prepared by Harrison Wright, Ph. D. Wilkes-Barre, 1883. 8vo., pp. 19. $0.25.

The Old Academy. Interesting sketch of its forty-six trustees. Harrison Wright, Ph. D. Broadside. 1883. $0.25.

Circular on Life Membership. 1884. 4to., p. 1.

Circular on the One Hundredth Anniversary of the Erection of Luzerne County.

Hon. Hendrick Bradley Wright. By Geo. B. Kulp. Wilkes-Barre, 1884. 8vo., pp. 12. No title page. Reprinted for the Society from Kulp's Families of Wyoming Valley.

An Account of Various Silver and Copper Medals presented to the North American Indians by the sovereigns of England, France and Spain, from 1600 to 1800, and especially of five such medals of George I. of Great Britain, now in the possession of the Society, and its members. Read before the Society September 12, 1885, by Rev. Horace Edwin Hayden, M. A., Curator of Numismatics. Wilkes-Barre, 1886. 8vo., pp. 26. Reprinted from vol. 2, part II. of the proceedings. $1.00

Ebenezer Warren Sturdevant. By George B. Kulp. Wilkes-Barre, 1884. 8vo., pp. 10. Reprinted for the Society from Kulp's Families of Wyoming Valley.

A Bibliography of the Wyoming Valley, Pennsylvania. Being a catalogue of all books, pamphlets and other ephemera in any way relating to its history, with bibliographical and critical notes, etc. Part I, by the Rev. Horace Edwin Hayden, A. M. Read before the Society December 14, 1883, and reprinted from vol. 2, part I, proceedings. Wilkes-Barre, 1886. 8vo., pp. 100. $1.00.

A Brief Review of the Literary Work of the late Harrison Wright, Ph. D., Recording Secretary and one of the Trustees of the Wyoming Historical and Geological Society. By Sheldon Reynolds. Wilkes-Barre, 1886. 8vo., pp. (2), 81-93. Reprinted from vol. 3 of the Proceedings and Collections of the Wyoming Historical and Geological Society.

Local Shell Beds. A paper read before the Society September 14, 1883, by Sheldon Reynolds, M. A. Reprinted from part I, volume 2, of the Proceedings and Collections of the Society. Wilkes-Barre, 1886. 8vo., pp. 10.

Report on some Fossils from the lower coal measures near Wilkes-Barre, Luzerne county, Pennsylvania. A paper read before the Society December 12, 1884, by Prof. E. W. Claypole. Reprinted from vol. 2, part II, of the Proceedings of the Society. Wilkes-Barre, Pa., 1886. 8vo., pp. 15.

Report on some Fossils from the lower coal measures near Wilkes-Barre, Luzerne county, Pennsylvania. By Prof. E. W. Claypole. From the Proceedings and Collections of the Society, Vol. 2, part II. Wilkes-Barre, 1886. 8vo., pp. 239-253.

Report on the Wyoming Valley Carboniferous Limestone Beds. By Charles A. Ashburner, geologist in charge of the anthracite survey, etc. Accompanied by a description of the fossils contained in the beds. By Angelo Heilprin. From the Proceedings of the Society, vol. 2, part II. Wilkes-Barre, 1886. 8vo., pp. 254-277. These two have printed titles on covers.

The Rev. Bernard Page, A. M., first Episcopal minister of Wyoming, A. D. 1771. Read before the Society September 12, 1884, by Sheldon Reynolds, M. A. Reprinted from part II, vol. 2, of the Proceedings and Collections of the Society. Wilkes-Barre, 1886. 8vo., pp. 13.

A Biographical Sketch of the late Hon. Edmund Lovell Dana, President of the Osterhout Free Library, Wilkes-Barre, Pa. By Sheldon Reynolds, M. A., Secretary. Prepared at the request of, and read before the directors of the library July 26, 1889, and before the Wyoming Historical and Geological Society September 13, 1889. Wilkes Barre, Pa., 1889. 8vo., pp. 11.

Coal, its Antiquity. Discovery and early development in the Wyoming Valley. A paper read before the Society June 27, 1890, by Geo. B. Kulp, Historiographer of the Society, Wilkes-Barre, 1890. Seal. 8vo., pp. 27.

The Massacre of Wyoming. The Acts of Congress for the defense of the Wyoming Valley, Pennsylvania, 1776-1778; with the Petitions of the Sufferers by the Massacre of July 3, 1778, for Congressional aid. With an introductory chapter by Rev. Horace Edwin Hayden, M. A., Corresponding Secretary Wyoming Histori cal and Geological Society. Seal. 8vo., frontispiece, pp. 119. Printed for the Society. Wilkes-Barre, Pa., 1895. $1.50.

Notes on the Tornado of August 19, 1890, in Luzerne and Columbia counties. A paper read before the Wyoming Historical and Geological Society December 12, 1890, by Prof. Thomas Santee, Principal of the Central High School. Seal. 8vo., pp. 51. Map. Wilkes-Barre, Pa., 1891. $1.00.

In Its New Home. The Wyoming Historical and Geological Society takes formal possession of its new quarters. Address of Hon. Stanley Woodward. From the *Evening Leader* Tuesday, November 21, 1893. 8vo., pp. 4.

Pedigree Building. Dr. William H. Egle. 1896. pp. 4.

The Yankee and the Pennamite in the Wyoming Valley. Hon. Stanley Woodward. 1896. pp. 4.

The Frontier Forts within the Wyoming Valley, Pennsylvania. A report of the Commission appointed by the State to mark the Forts erected against the Indians prior to 1783, by Sheldon Reynolds, M. A., a Member of the Commission, and president of the Wyoming Historical and Geological Society. With a brief memoir of the author, by Andrew H. McClintock, M. A. Read before the Wyoming Historical and Geological Society December, 1894, and reprinted from the State Report, 1896. Seal. Wilkes-Barre, Penn'a, 1896. 8vo., pp. 48. Illustrations. $1.00.

The Frontier Forts within the North and West Branches of the Susquehanna River, Pennsylvania. A Report of the Commission appointed by the State to mark the Frontier Forts erected against the Indians prior to 1783, by Captain John M. Buckalew, a Member of the Commission, and Corresponding Member of the Wyoming Historical and Geological Society. Read before the Society October 4, 1895, and reprinted from the State Report, 1896. Seal. Wilkes-Barre, Penn'a, 1896. 8vo., pp. 70. Illustrations. $1.00.

www.ingramcontent.com/pod-product-compliance
Lightning Source LLC
Chambersburg PA
CBHW020310090426
42735CB00009B/1298